KOREAN WORKS AND DAYS

事記時鄉城鐸權司域

父神榮大盧

KOREAN
WORKS AND DAYS

NOTES FROM THE DIARY
OF A COUNTRY PRIEST

BY RICHARD RUTT

KOREA BRANCH
ROYAL ASIATIC SOCIETY

Reprinted 1978

*Layout & typography
by Ken Tremayne*

Printed in Korea

REGINAE
CARMELI
DECORI

*Strip to sow and strip to plow and strip to reap
if you wish to garner all Demeter's fruits in due
season, so that each may grow in order. Else
afterwards you may chance to want . . .*

Hesiod: Works and Days

CONTENTS

Contents

PREFACE

THIS BOOK is based on a series of articles about Korean village life which I wrote in 1957 and 1958 for the daily *Korea Times,* the only independent English-language newspaper in Seoul. Although the articles have been expanded, adapted, and re-edited for publication in book form, they still do not pretend to be more than occasional reflections and impressions of Korean country life, and many interesting customs and important factors have not been described.

The original articles were published anonymously without any identifications of the places or people mentioned, though their authorship was an open secret among readers of the paper. In their new form they owe much to the generous and careful advice on their editing and presentation which I received from Mrs Kurt Mattusch.

It seemed best not to introduce many proper names into these notes, even in book form. We do not use many names in village conversation, except for places. To most English readers the insertion of many unfamiliar Korean names would be merely irritating, so I have left things as they were. In a few places I have translated village names; in those cases I think the English version conveys fairly accurately the impression which the Korean name gives to the native speaker.

But there is no longer any point in not identifying the locality described. It is a peninsula on the west coast, about sixty miles south of Seoul, in the county of P'yŏngt'aek,

Kyŏnggi Province, and the village in which I lived was Anjung.

The poems at the head of each section of the book are translations of *sijo*, the highly sophisticated three-line songs of old Korea. That so many of them sing of country life speaks eloquently of the essentially rural character of Korean culture.

The fact that I ever wrote about my country parish and its people was entirely due to the then editor of the *Korea Times*, Choi Byungwoo. His death by drowning (or so we must presume) off Quemoy, where he was covering the little war there on his way home from Indonesia in September, 1958, was a great loss to Korea as well as to Korean journalism. If there is any perception in these accounts of country life, it is in great part due to him. To many foreign readers it was the exotic and the quaint in the articles that appealed; to Byungwoo it was the facts, and above all the precise facts, of a rural community poised between the old dispensation and the new, as well as the clear country air, that made these pieces worth while.

These are the two most important things to me even now: the people and the atmosphere. Chief among the people was Yi Yongjik, the scholar with whom I walked so many miles and from whom I learned how Chinese poetry is written and all the rural vocabulary I know—slow in most of his thoughts and speech, distressingly poor, but courteous and with a charming sense of humour. He was Elijah the catechist.

Then there was Michael, my teen-age houseboy, Man'gil in Korean, and Mangdungi (Mudfish) to his contemporaries. He sharpened my eyes to many things and kept me well informed in his broad dialect speech. Of course there were many others, and some of them real friends. Yet the memory of Anjung is a memory of a community rather than of individuals, a hardworking community, buzzing with rumours, but a community that when it relaxed, relaxed completely.

And of the atmosphere in which they live it is the smells

rather than the sights that remain as a nostalgic legacy: not only the cesspool and the pigsty, the *kimch'i* and the fermented soy that permeate the back alleys, but the sweet smell of pine smoke at morning and evening, the wholesome smell of stored grain, the pungent sesame, and the fragrance of rice flowers or pinewoods under a summer sun. All those, with June's dust, July's dank vegetation, January's scentless winds, and the clinging smell of the fish market. But always and everywhere the odour of the good red earth.

Seoul
August 1960   R.R.

Preface to the second edition

Although Korean tradition is tenacious, much has changed since this book was written. The 'New Village Movement' has even changed the appearance of the countryside, to the detriment of its visual charm where it has banished the elephant-grey thatch and replaced it with brightly painted metal or asbestos roofing, but to the great benefit of the villagers, the quality of whose life is much improved where ditches have been lined with stone-work and walls made sound with concrete blocks. Communications are also greatly improved, and most hamlets now have electric light. Rural medical services are not ideal, but they are better, and it would now be possible, whereas fifteen years ago it was not, to arrange psychiatric care for a demented girl.

Some of the old customs, as I predicted, are now subjects for studious preservation by learned societies, and it would be hard to find a folk perfomance of a puppet play in a village square. Folklore is now seen as a national asset, and though the farmers' dances have been turned into modern stage extravaganzas performed by troupes of girls, they still survive in their

13

true masculine form in the villages and agricultural schools. Buddhism has had an impressive intellectual renascence and counts for more than it did in the life of the nation, yet I doubt whether its renewed vigour has yet penetrated to the country-side. If I wrote today of Korean Christianity, however, I should have little different to say. Like Buddhism, Christianity has raised its intellectual power; there is now professional ecumenical activity at the top leadership levels; and the days when material relief from overseas was so important in church life are almost forgotten. In spite of thankfulness for these and other advances, I still believe that the spiritual problems with which the Korean churches have to grapple are the ones I sensed in Anjung. My chief cause for thankfulness is the improved relations between christians and buddhists: my own respect for Korean Buddhism is much greater than when I wrote of the little temples of my country parish.

In preparing this edition I have tidied up the syntax and punctuation, improved the romanizations and reorganized the paragraphs. I have corrected a few details relating to botany and other peripheral subjects, but have resisted the temptation to add new information. The book is an account of Kyŏnggi-do villages in the late fifties, and reflects what I saw and knew then, not what I see and know now. I am glad to take the opportunity of noting here, however, that the authorship and dating of the *sijo* poems given in this book is traditional and should be taken as such. There is no firm evidence to prove that in their present form the poems are older than the eighteen th century.

I should also like to acknowledge that the title of the book and the reference to Hesiod were suggested by Mr Meredith Weatherby.

Taejon
Michaelmas 1973

KOREAN WORKS AND DAYS

In hempen shorts, with stubby hoes,
  we went to weed the rice fields;
Shouting songs that farmers sing,
  we came back when the moon was up.
The housewife dishes out the wine:
  There's the back field to do tomorrow, she reminds.

Sin Hŭimun (ca 1800?)

OUR VILLAGE

郷

黨

IT IS STILL a source of surprise to me that a country so well known to the West as Korea now is should be so inaccurately known. Almost any book on Korean life which you may pick up will have misstatements great or small—the astonishing Osgood being an honourable exception. Generally speaking, there seem to be two main branches of error. The first describes Korea as though she were still living in the Yi dynasty, giving a romantic picture of an exotic land. The second describes an entirely modernized and westernized country that does not exist outside Seoul, Pusan, and Taegu.

But perhaps writers about Korea are not to be blamed too harshly. Most of us foreigners see little beyond Seoul and some one other corner of the country. A cursory ride through the provinces should be enough to show that there are few generalizations about contemporary Korea that can be valid. The life of a village in Kangwŏn Province, where the peasants eke out a scanty living from stone-strewn barley fields, and roof their houses with untrimmed slate held down by lumps of rock, is obviously not the same as the life of the luxurious rice valleys of Kanghwa Island, with its thickly thatched roofs, its orchards, and its vineyards. And what a gulf exists between the small, albeit influential, minority of sophisticated city dwellers and the great majority of Koreans, who are farmers with a very different degree of knowledge of Western culture.

17

From province to province the customs are different. In my parish few old men ever wear the traditional Korean black hat. Its yellow counterpart for mourning and the widest kind of mourning hat seem to have disappeared completely, though the big practical rain-hat of split and plaited straw is still in use. Yet a short while ago I spent a few days farther south in Ch'ungch'ŏng Province; the black hat was common, and mourning hats were easy to see—in fact there were big piles of them in the shops.

No aspect of contemporary Korean life is more fascinating for either the Korean or the Western observer to study than the varying degrees to which traditional customs are continuing to hold out in some areas but disappearing in others, with corresponding variations in the degree to which Western culture has really infiltrated the people's lives. And part of such study will involve the exact degree to which the temper of Seoul really represents or influences the temper of the rest of the country. The rest of the country is numerically the vast majority. The most intriguing question of all is the exact force of that word 'numerically'.

Our village is Anjung, the market centre of a rhomboidal peninsula on the north shore of the Asan Gulf, known to the nineteenth-century hydrographers as Prince Jerome's Gulf. I sit on Beacon Hill of an evening and look across the smooth water to the blue mountains of Ch'ungch'ŏng Province and wonder who Prince Jerome was and how his name got fixed to this coast.

Beacon Hill is a good place to see the area from. You can see the whole peninsula, with all its hilly headlands creeping out into the Yellow Sea in the west, the shining gulf to the south, and the flat rice fields going off to the east towards P'yŏngt'aek, where the American air-base lights twinkle in the evenings; while the whitish roads wind over the hills to the north on the way to Suwŏn, and ultimately to Seoul, the capital. Those roads are modern, made by the Japanese; but in the hills toward Suwŏn you can occasionally see cuttings for broad, grassy tracks where the old Korean roads used to go. It was those old roads that gave Anjung its name.

Until three generations ago here was only a nodal point where the roads from the little peninsula met up with the main track to the capital that led up from the ferry crossing the gulf from the south. (There is still a deal of local traffic this way.) At the junction of the roads was a great tree and a wine-shop, providing a place to sit down and rest: in Korean, *anjui*. The old name still clings in that form to a little hamlet nearby where the people make earthenware crocks; like so many of their trade in Korea, they are Roman catholics. The form *anjung* comes from the transliteration of *anjui* into Chinese characters. The *an* means peace, but the *jung* means 'second'. It was chosen because the true Korean word for 'second in order' is a rough pun on the word for 'resting place'. There are many rural verbal games in Korean place names.

Nowadays there are three hundred houses in the village, and nearly everybody lives off the local mixed agriculture, especially rice, barley, and root crops. Fruit is not important, and there is not much fishing this side of the gulf, but chicken-rearing is a developing industry. The salterns which the Japanese developed in the neighbourhood are being extended, and it is there that the refugees from North Korea are mostly working—the lucky and successful ones, that is, for many are still living in miserable houses, living by such trades as making matchboxes, or cheap fans of paper and split bamboo.

Anjung itself depends on its market and its schools, of which there are three. Its trade has about reached saturation point: several new businesses have failed recently. But the villages scattered among the hills and woods have not a shop between them; they depend on the shallowly terraced paddies

19

that are so painstakingly tended and flooded every year to produce a high yield of Asia's finest-quality rice, and on the woods and mountainsides that provide the essential fuel for the fierce winter.

Beacon Hill stands just outside the west end of the village and is half quarried away for its soft white stone. It is the highest hill nearby, except for Mai Hill (the name seems to be one of Korea's many corruptions of the Sanskrit word for jewel), a couple of miles to the north. The highest point in the village is very near the foot of the hill and is crowned by the tiny shrine of the tutelary spirit of the place, backed by its thin screen of untidy trees. The next hill is crowned by my church, a long Korean hall with proudly curving eaves that floats over the village like the great mystic ship that it stands for and has a horizontal name board over the door whose modest Chinese inscription proclaims: 'The Holy Temple of the Lord of Heaven'.

Along the south side of the church the main street runs eastwards, flanked by the chief shops, all of which have their fronts open to the dust of the street and are also used as meeting places for neighbourly chats. Some are specialized trades, like the carpenter, the butcher, the oilman, the cycle mender, and the eating houses; but most are general stores selling everything from cheap brooches to hard soap, garlic, matches, and bottled rice spirits. At the far end of the street is the bus stop, where the roads divide and the roofs run beside them down the hillside to the new grain market, a great open space at the bottom; or out towards the large galvanized metal county granary and the little thatched church of the Nazarene Mission, the other side of the fish market, which has fish in it only on the regular market days.

Most of the roofs are thatched. Some, like mine, are of painted corrugated iron. A few well-to-do old families have the much-respected tiles. But by and large the village still lives under what they call 'grass roofs'.

The Korean house is interesting, and since so many aspects of it do not have a ready name in English it will be worth while to describe it. Our village houses differ very much in size, but almost without exception they have thick wattle-and-daub walls or are simply built of large blocks of dried mud, faced with an ochreous mud plaster. In English terms, they are thatched cottages. Doors and windows are mostly of white paper pasted on wooden frames, and the doors that lead outside are generally on iron hinges. The sills and thresholds are high, to prevent draughts for people sleeping on the floor. Inside doors slide in grooves.

The plan of the typical house is L-shaped. In the angle of the L is the largest room, the living room of the family. It has the famous *ondol* or hot floor, built by making flues under a floor of stone and mud. The floor is finished with several layers of oiled yellow paper, which darkens with age and the heat of the flues, sometimes to a warm russet colour.

The furniture is generally only a chest or two and a few cushions, with a tiny writing table. The main cupboards are let into the wall, a large one for bedding and a smaller one for medicines, tobacco, food dainties, and the like. The walls are generally covered with cheap wallpaper, sometimes with newspaper or other scrap, really intended as an undercoat. The ceiling may be of paper pasted on a grid of stretched string—if it is, the rats will live on it and run round with a thunderous din on the taut paper. (Some people let small pieces of glass into the ceiling so that the rat will think there is a hole and be stopped short in his longer and louder runs, but it doesn't seem to help much. You have to get used to sleeping with the noise.) Or the beams of the ceiling may be those of the roof.

The fireplace, over which the floor is too hot to sit on but is the proper place for a guest, is seen and fed in the kitchen, which is next to the living room in one arm of the L. It has an earth floor, much lower than the other rooms of the house.

There is a chopping board and a cupboard or two for crocks; little meal-tables hang from the walls or ceiling; there are one or two cauldrons built into the fireplace, so that the fuel that cooks the food also heats the living-room floor. Beyond the kitchen, at the end of this arm of the L, is the fuel store, and possibly the cowhouse.

On the other side of the living room is a space which is open on the courtyard. This has a wooden floor and is called the *maru* in Korean, the ceremonial meeting-place of the household, which for want of a better word I call verandah in English. Shoes are kicked off before one steps on to it. Here are the big rice-chests and here, generally, are the shrines for the tablets of the recently dead, and on the rafters the inscription about the date of building the house. Photographs may be displayed there. It is a fine place to sit—under the shade of its roof—in the hot summer days.

Beyond it, finishing the second arm of the L, is another hot-floored room. Sometimes this is the men's parlour or study. It has another door on the outside, and is the place for receiving male guests, but very often in these days it is the room for the married son and is called the 'bride's room'. If it is so used, you can be sure to find in it a miniature dressing-table with a mirror and many cosmetics; some ugly cheap modern chests and wardrobes; and the bridegroom's suits hanging on the wall under white linen covers with bright satin-stitch embroidery which often proclaims: 'Home Sweet Home' in florid English lettering. And, of course, a photo of a poker-faced wedding group. But if it is the men's parlour, then there will be one door to the outside world (nearby is an elemental urinal) and one door to the yard, to which the womenfolk bring the wine and food; inside it will be very bare, but there may be a few books and cushions and probably a straw mat on the floor.

The sexes are still very much segregated, even for sleeping, when the quilts and mattresses are simply taken from the cupboards and unrolled across the floor of the dayrooms. At mealtimes the men are fed at little tables on the verandah or hot floor. The women eat afterwards in the living room or kitchen. Children often eat separately from adults, or at least at different tables.

Larger houses have two L-shaped blocks, almost enclosing a square. Behind the living room is the garden where the pickle jars and vats are kept, with the well and a few fruit-trees and plants. This is the women's preserve, and here the spirits of the site have their home. There is a thick earth wall around the property, but the great gate, with its double doors, opens on to an unwalled yard of beaten earth in front of the house, where the threshing is done and grain is spread to dry in the autumn. The men's parlour is always in the front block and its outside door gives on to this yard.

Of course there are many variations—some houses are smaller and some very much larger but this is the basic pattern. Few and far between, these days, in the Anjung area, are the great houses with summer arbours in the garden and fish ponds. The chief difference now from house to house is merely a matter of size.

The most distinctive thing about any house anywhere is its smell. Korean country houses smell of wood smoke, grain, and pickles. It is a wholesome smell and, once you become used to it, a very comforting one. There is no obvious luxury or even decoration in the farmers' houses. Always a calendar pasted on the wall; sometimes a Japanese clock, maybe no longer working or very much off time (it doesn't matter anyway); a number of small snapshots, arranged in one frame, hang at an angle very near the ceiling so as to be seen easily by those sitting on the floor; maybe some pressed leaves pasted between the layers of paper in the window to give a decorative silhouette.. . . All the ornaments of the unsophisticated who yet belong to a great culture.

The farmer is in fact the heart of Korean culture, which has, broadly speaking, only two facets, the aristocratic taste of the capital and the peasant culture of the provinces. Unlike Japan, which has had an important merchant class for several centuries, Korea has scarcely yet developed that urban middle class which alone can produce a bourgeois culture—the world of fashion and the theatre, of popular music and widespread reading of fiction. The tastes of the educated farmer have percolated down from the palace along with Chinese literature. The tastes and prejudices of the uneducated countryman reflect the deep Northeast Asian substrata of the Korean race, born in shamanastic tribal life and transmogrified by the life of agricultural peasants.

Korean arts are beginning to be understood and known, but a proper appreciation of Korean culture must await adequate research into Korea's social history, which remains yet to be done. Nevertheless, this much is clear: Korea is profoundly different from Japan in almost every respect. She was never truly feudal, with an aristocracy rooted to its local soil; she was never imperially independent of China, even in her own eyes; but above all she was never urbanized, and even today the Korean mind is fundamentally a rural mind. In many respects she is enviable.

春

SPRING

The pale dawn lights the eastern window,
  already larks are singing in the sky.
Little boy cowherd,
  how comes it that you are not up?
In that field over the hilltop,
  when will you get those furrows ploughed?

Nam Kuman (1651–1733)

FEBRUARY

新
元

'SPRING begins' (Ipch'un) says the traditional calendar at this time. We have exchanged the rigours of the cold for the discomforts of the thaw. 'Tis true that I look up from my desk to see fields and mountains still white with snow, but the whiteness no longer dazzles the eyes, because the roofs of the houses are now white only on the north side, and the trees and paths are all free of snow, so the snowscape is broken by many dark spots and the pinewoods show again as a solid green mass.

The paths may be free of snow, but they are not any easier to walk along. They are thick in squelching mud. Galoshes are a necessity, and every time I go out I come back well spattered with our famous red earth. Every alleyway is noisy with the constant drip of water from the eaves. The morning frost is welcome because it makes everywhere less wet; but on the dry verandahs of the houses facing south, people are sitting to chat as though spring were fully come.

The 'Beginning of Spring' day was traditionally the day for renewing the inscriptions outside the houses. It was especially appropriate to paste up a strip of paper saying 'The Beginning of Spring Is a Great Joy', and on the other half of the double door would go a pendant verse saying 'The Coming of the Sunshine Brings Many Blessings'. These are still to be seen on some doors in the village, but I doubt whether many will have been renewed this year.

More common on the great gates of houses are the characters for the dragon and the tiger, representing beneficent astrological influences. They may be expanded into four-character phrases declaring that the dragon, representing life and growth, brings the Five Blessings (Longevity, Riches, Harmony, Virtue, Finishing the Allotted Span); while the tiger chases away the Three Disasters: thieves, fire, and ghosts. But occasionally one sees more literary expressions, such as 'Tortoise and Lotus' on one door and 'Ducks and Duckweed' on the other. The tortoise character invokes longevity, and the lotus the blessings to go with it. Ducks and duckweed suggest domestic contentment, and in Korea that involves ducklings as well as duck.

Comparatively few houses carry any inscriptions on the beams and pillars inside. Not many people practise calligraphy these days. Sometimes a yellowed and faded set of characters may still linger over the outside door of the menfolks' parlour, but there is rarely anything more. Occasionally these texts have all the startling effectiveness of a modern poster, as in one village I know where the eye is caught and rivetted by four huge characters on a house-front proclaiming that 'Virtue Alone Is Truly Precious'. These texts, inside or over studies, are not as a rule astrological. They tend to be inspirational, though not always classic, quotations. They may be composed by someone in the family, or a friend, much as elegiac verses were exchanged and inscribed in the days when Europe had a flourishing culture of literary urbanity. Nowadays one even occasionally sees printed facsimiles of calligraphy in people's houses.

But whatever other writings may be missing in a house, if it is at all self-respecting it will have an inscription on the main roof-beam. This inscription always sets out in detail the day and hour when the beam was erected, together with the birth date of the master of the house, and the description of the compass direction which the house faces. This is all done, not in plain figures, but with the sixty combinations of horary Chinese characters, which are used for both dates and directions. The system is by no means as complicated as it looks at first. It bears relation, of course, to the old system of choosing a grave site, and all bespeaks a great effort to live in harmony with the forces of nature. The odd feature of the inscription is that the master of the house referred to in it is always the eldest son of the youngest generation of the family. Presumably he is likely to last longest, so the inscription is prenamed, as it were.

At the ends of the beam there are almost invariably the characters of the dragon and the phoenix, and sometimes the tortoise and the griffin as well. These are the four mystic creatures of legend, and do not belong to the astrological system. (The tiger does, but he was not mystical in old Korea; he was real.) The phoenix is a marital symbol because Oriental phoenixes go in pairs, and the Oriental dragon is a beneficent spirit.

Christian houses sometimes adapt their house inscriptions to fit their faith, with varying degrees of literary success. Not long ago I was in a protestant house which had a revolutionized legend on the roof beam, with all the figures and dates modernized and a Christian prayer interwoven. Yet I noted that the dragon and the phoenix characters were still nestling quietly in the shadows at the very ends of the beam. And indeed, why should not such rich and healthy symbols as these be baptized?

29

MARCH

春
和

ONE OF THE lads came in excitedly the other evening, insisting that I go with him to see a film. There are often film shows in the village, brought round by a team with a van and a travelling screen and projector. An area by one of the big granaries is staked off with tall poles, and cotton sheeting is stretched between them. The floor space is covered with heavy grain mats, and the audience jostles for a space to sit down. Nobody sits still for long, and so the audience is continually moving. There are frequent stops in the showing and these not only when they change the reels. The charge for entrance is 100 hwan (roughly sixpence or ten cents) a head, but my young friend insisted that I should both be let in free and given a chair when I got there. It was chilly for all that.

The film was a fairly well-worn copy and a fairly old one of the story of Sim Ch'ŏng, the filial daughter who gave all to restore the sight of her blinded father. It is a favourite old Korean tale. Much of the photography was sensitive, and some of the direction was appealing, but, as usual, the pace was very slow for Western taste.

I enjoyed most the scene where Sim Ch'ŏng went to the bottom of the sea to become a slave in the Dragon King's Palace. It was not the slightly Egyptianesque set used in the film that gave pleasure, but the children in the audience. For this sequence the dialogue fell into the old courtly language, solemn and flowery, such as is nowadays heard only in prayers.

Every time the Dragon King ended a speech with a sonorous inflexion, all the children present chorused back a delighted 'A-men!'.

It takes a long time to run through a film like this, and no supporting features are offered. Thoroughly numbed, we walked back up the village street. The pleasant sound of the old-fashioned ironing sticks beating on the ironing stones sounded from many of the houses, but for the most part the village is quiet after dark. Then all through the night we hear the clack, clack, of the two ironing sticks carried by the night-watch patrolman. The noise is supposed to let us know that all is well. It serves just as much to warn thieves and other rascals when to make themselves scarce.

APRIL

花

雨

SPRING was long delayed, but it really broke in our village on Holy Saturday. As I went over to the church for the Paschal Vigil service, late in the evening, I first heard the chorus of the frogs in the paddy fields, that steady shimmering crackle that dominates every other impression of a Korean summer night. As the noise came through the church windows it made a good ground bass for the gay cacophony of our bells at the first Easter Gloria. During the week the annual parable of the resurrection got properly under way. The yellow forsythia, triumphant but rather vulgar, was out first. Then the apricot blossoms crowned the village with their snowy glory. The hills took up the theme in a minor key with purple azalea, violets, and tiny irises. Last of all, and loveliest, the magenta peach blossom transformed every hamlet that possessed it.

Field work has gathered momentum with the increase of the flowers. The last of the spring house-building is practically finished now (even the church repairs are nearly done), and only a few very old men are still busy with any of the many and various jobs of straw-plaiting which have been going on through most of the winter. Many of the farmers are out in the fields. We have a large very flat area where the treadmills for moving water from one level to another have been consistently busy for nearly a month now, and the vents of the Irrigation Co-operative's pipes seem always to be gushing water into the fields. Women, and even children, are working here and there with that slowest-looking of all Korean aids to irrigation, the boat-shaped scoop suspended from a tall tripod.

Walking on the baulks or turfed ridges between the paddies is dangerous and unpleasant since the men are digging out the edges of the fields and throwing the silt up on to the paths. In mud up to their calves, they are still preparing seedbeds for the rice, though many of the prepared beds are already green with the first tips of the seedlings.

Yet the tempo of village life has still not the tension of the busiest seasons of the year—transplanting and reaping times. The spring air is also a sleepy air, and there is a self-conscious enjoyment of the sun. Hence this is the peak of the picnic season. I had understood that the English were peculiarly devoted to picnics, but the Koreans will scarcely render first place to anyone in appreciation of the alfresco party. We have had several in the parish recently. The ingredients are always the same: a pleasant spot, a wealth of food, including a large supply of leather-tough dried squid, plenty of children, the picking of wild flowers, and the inevitable singing at the end.

Our parish parties have a pleasant variation. We have two learned gentlemen of the old school who never miss any parochial function and have their own ways of extracting further enjoyment from any occasion. They will crack jokes with the youngest present, but they will also amuse themselves by testing their knowledge of the literary Chinese names for common wild flowers. Once a sophisticated youth brought bananas fresh from Seoul to the picnic. 'What', asked the scholar, by way of entertainment, 'is the Chinese literary word for banana?'

Before we leave for home, and probably after their noon-day nap, these two gentlemen will produce a piece of paper—a scrap of waste or a cigarette carton—and one of them will propose a rhyme syllable, on the basis of which they will proceed to a competition in making a classical Chinese ode to suit the occasion. I am still amazed at the speed with which they are able to compose correctly and appositely in the complex rhyme and tone pattern of strict T'ang prosody, with or without a smattering of classical allusions and quotations. If they were Chinese it would still appear very efficient, but since they are Koreans, for whom the tones of Chinese have purely academic significance, I find their feat considerable. So far I have not caught them indulging in more cliché than English occasional verse is liable to contain; but although their productions are explained to us afterwards with a wealth of searching critical detail, I am reliant on their own evaluation of their achievements when considered as literature. I am better fitted to enjoy the short couplets, quips, and quotations which fall from their conversation like sparks from an anvil at all times and in all places.

One of these two men is Elijah, who teaches Chinese characters and a little elementary classical grammar in the local middle school. It is the most normal thing in the world for young folk to say, 'We do not know any Chinese', and for the schoolboys to complain that it is difficult to learn, but their pride in the knowledge of their teacher is surely no less than it would have been in the days when all Korean education was in Chinese. The whole country-side points with pride to a beautiful example of his writing engraved in a memorial kiosk beside one of our main roads, and everyone knows him under the name of 'the Chinese teacher'. To walk with him from one village to another is to have your conversation constantly interrupted by schoolboys dismounting from their bicycles to bow and doff their caps to him. Yet he is not an old man. He is barely fifty. He tells me that there used to be gatherings of the literati for poetry parties, where wine and good food were provided and a rhyme character proposed, on the basis of which all present composed a poem. Many of the old participants are dead, and there are few who think it worth while to arrange such parties nowadays: the side issues of our

Sunday school picnics are the tail end of a great tradition.

Yet the tradition still has some kick left in it. Soon after the Sunday-school party, one Kong, of a village near the gulf, arranged such a poetry party in his village, on a rounded hill called Jade Fairy Peak. It was a pleasant place, all covered with the short tough Korean turf. The proverbial spring winds were blowing gustily, and the little tents and awnings flapped continuously. Throughout the morning the white-coated men, about seventy of them in all, continued to arrive, walking over the bare rice fields in straggly little groups. Women and boys were struggling up the hillside with huge saucepans of peppery stew and buckets of wine. We sat on the straw mats under the awnings and ate quantities of delicious raw fish, red and juicy, accompanied by aromatic sprigs of the garden artemisia dipped in a mild red-pepper sauce. This is poets' food indeed, especially when washed down with draughts of clear golden rice wine.

The rhyme characters set for the meeting meant open, cup, come, terrace, and urge. In the regular eight-line stanza of the poem there are fixed places where these rhymes must appear; and all the poems had to deal with the scenery of the Jade Fairy Mountain and the present meeting. Unlike the old days, the rhyme characters had been announced beforehand, and many came bringing their compositions with them. Some, it was rumoured, had been ghosted. Elijah showed virtuosity by producing two poems, both meeting the standards set.

Under one of the awnings sat the scribe with the writing brush, surrounded by a group of the gentlemen and a floating cloud of boys, who were pupils of Mr Kong in the cottage school at the foot of the hill. One of the boys, looking very neat in a striking checked shirt, was grinding the ink-stick on the inkstone. The poets came up and chanted their compositions in the scribe's ear as they squatted beside him, and he wrote them quickly down on a seemingly endless scroll of paper. Pressed to contribute, I managed a brief quatrain about a single crow in a flight of cranes, which produced a hearty guffaw at my black suit among the white Korean coats and was well in tune with the atmosphere of the occasion.

The eating, the chatting, the poetasting went on until late in the afternoon, when lunch was served, and more cauldrons, this time full of steaming rice, were lugged up the hill. Finally the scroll was read over to the assembly— perhaps a rather monotonous anthology but a satisfactory *terminus ad quem* for a fine picnic.

Last week I was passing through a remote hill-girt village on my way to visit some of my farthest-flung parishioners. My old catechist companion, T'aekhwa, told me that in this village lived a scholar who had never cut his topknot, and he undertook to introduce me to him. T'aekhwa is a jolly old fellow, though by now desperately poor. He has a round and apple red face with a straggly white beard, and shining black eyes forever screwed up in a goblin's happy smile. On high days and holidays he comes out in a proper old Korean coat, white in summer and grey in winter, but at other times he is in cast-off Western clothing, usually with a pair of striped pants that combine with his jolly face to remind me of a minstrel-show character.

Yet he is a man of the old school, and is known to his literary friends as Kyo'un, Cloud Bridge. He knows a dozen words, maybe, of English. He has always tended to be a progressive, but he has great respect for this old patriarch of the Hyŏn clan and especially for his topknot. The Japanese government wanted them all removed because they symbolized the dignity of old-style Korean gentlemen. T'aekhwa lost his long ago, and now even if he wanted to grow it again, as some have done, he could not. His pate is smooth and round.

We came to the largest house in the village, neatly thatched and well repaired. The old man's reception room was a large one, with plenty of light coming softly through the paper windows, lighting up the yellow floor much as alabaster windows produce a warm golden light in a Romanesque church. The scholar sat on a white mattress at one end, pulling at a very long pipe. He had a thick, long beard and a gleaming silver topknot, well groomed and very large—one which claims never to have bowed before the Japanese.

That afternoon some of his sons and grandsons were gathered, collating material about the family tree for inclusion in the genealogy at the next meeting of the clan. The latest edition of the genealogy was there in three great yellow folio volumes. The old man asserted that their original forefather (it was not one of the greatest clans) had come from China with Ch'i Tzŭ, a thousand years before Christ; but the earliest name in the book was that of a Koryŏ man of the late Middle Ages, and the youngest person present belonged only to the twenty-sixth generation. This was an edition of some thirty years ago. There was copious introductory matter in Chinese, and some attractive plates showing maps of the chief burial sites of the clan, in some of which a railway cut an inappropriate gash through the dragon spurs of the hills and the attractive little drawings of pavilions and archive houses. There was a list of the characters proper to the names of each generation of the clan. The bulk of the book was the list of members of the family, with their dates, marriage details, familiar and official names, and, invariably, identifications of their graves.

Rice wine was brought in. (Rice wine is variable—this was oddly reminiscent of the dry white wines of central Italy.) In the course of normal polite conversation it was natural that the fact that I have no children should come to light. In the circumstances it was a striking fact. My host professed to be blankly puzzled. Then he even became impatient, and a little angry. Why am I not doing something about it? Have I no regard for my ancestors? But he did not overpass his manners, and we parted in peace. As we walked over the hills to the next village I wondered whether my friend's grandchildren will have the same difficulty in understanding the Westerner's disregard for descendants. Will they treasure their genealogies as historical documents? Or will they still treat them as instruments of filial piety? At least I hope that they will not forget them altogether.

There was an accident in our village last Monday. A heavy truck overturned and two young men were thrown beneath it and killed. I knew neither of the men, though I knew where one of them lived. The next night the sorceress had been called in, and throughout the dark hours the horrid clanging of her gong reminded the village of dead souls not at rest.

Yesterday I was passing along the road where the accident happened. It was late afternoon, and the air was damp. It was the time of the accident. A small group of chubby-faced schoolboys were dawdling on their way home, and one or two men had stopped while a group of women watched two sorceresses placating the spirits of the dead men. It was not a spectacular sight, but it was thoroughly horrifying. The two sorceresses, in plain, clean white clothes, were dancing gracelessly over the spot where the men had died. They waved bowls of boiled rice and fruit, dishes of well-dressed meat and other good food. They took the rice in their mouths, chewed it, and spat it out as they danced. They scattered the fruit and other food in all directions. There was constant banging of the gong in a hypnotic rhythm, and a mumbo-jumbo of inarticulate words from the two dancers.

One of the widows was there. Sometimes she struck the gong herself, sometimes one of the sorceresses came up to her and stood swaying in front of her, chanting in her face. The poor woman was in a coma. She swayed and seemed likely to fall over, but her friends supported her. Her eyes were open, but her irises quite disappeared beneath her upper eyelids. There was a business-like demeanour about the two sorceresses. They showed no signs of rapture: they had an impressive

39

bundle of green 100-hwan notes which they sometimes waved in the dancing. Occasionally one of them fell out and spoke to the bystanders. They were two rather handsome women. Almost suddenly it seemed that all the food had been cast away. I did not see exactly how it ended, and I do not know how they used the bundle of paper ribbons which seems to be the sorceress's trademark. The widow gained control of herself and led the party back towards the village.

Will they now believe that we have no reason to fear the spirits of these unfortunate men? A man near the place told me that the spirits of the young who die suddenly need special placating. 'We have to do this,' he said. And he laughed.

If ever I collected Korean folk-tales, I should call the collection 'The Tiger and the Toilet Shed', for surely no other two things are so powerfully evocative of dramatic situations in the folk mind of Korea. Indeed a six-year-old girl once sat with me on the verandah and generously offered to tell me a story. It was all about a tiger having trouble with a toilet shed. I soon lost the thread, but I caught the spirit of her breathless narration. We have little experience of tigers here, but plenty of toilet sheds. When our orphanage has an entertainment we expect at least one sketch to be centred on a door clearly marked 'Toilet'. The joke is generally connected with the lengthy occupation of the place, although it is not, as an early Japanese traveller noted of American toilets, 'customary to take a book there.' I have had people tell me pieces of information gleaned from scanning the pieces of newspaper provided, but this is rare. Most country people do not use paper; they collect a handful of straw from the stack on their way to the place.

The wooden slats across the top of a sometimes very large cesspit would seem to be no encouragement for unnecessary sojourning, but I saw a very amusing mime done by some Roman catholic altar-boys which assumed that some do stay overlong. A drunk entered and then hung his scarf over the door. When he left he forgot his scarf. The next comer saw the scarf, assumed the place engaged and waited in discomfort. A small queue formed, in mounting agony. A policeman joined them and was given priority. A National Assemblyman went right to the front of the queue. The audience, including a Korean nun, was in tucks until the drunk returned to collect his scarf.

Of course, the sufferers should have coughed. You cough as you approach the door. If anyone is inside, he coughs back, and you wait. I know a bishop who kept getting answering coughs again and again for a long time before he realized that he was being answered by a pig in the sty next door.

The countryside in spring is naturally idyllic. The sunshine is bright but pale; the skylarks sing their hearts out as they hover above, seemingly suspended from the blue ceiling. The only other sound in the valleys is the 'Do-do-do!' of the ploughman controlling his patient cow while her newly-born calf scampers along beside her, scrambling over the baulks and tripping in the furrows. This odd call seems to be the only command the ploughman ever gives his beast. It is meant to call her back from her veering course, for she habitually lurches.

Yesterday I took the Blessed Sacrament to a sick man who lives at Songdam, a pleasant hamlet nestling in a leafy dell. It was just such an idyllic morning. The sick man was on the verandah of the little farmhouse so that he might at least take some pleasure from the sunlight and air. As we knelt around the tiny table and prayed, a pair of swallows were busily chattering away as they remade their nests under a beam of the low ceiling, almost brushing our heads with their rapid wingstrokes. The family had tacked pieces of cardboard under the nesting place to catch the droppings, and the two swallows perched and prattled there fearlessly, well within reach of everybody's hands.

> This guest of summer,
> The temple-haunting martlet, does approve
> By his lov'd mansionry, that the heavens' breath
> Smells wooingly here.

For the Koreans as well as for Shakespeare, nesting swallows are a happy omen, and the people like to have them set their 'pendent bed and procreant cradle' inside the houses. Shakespeare's auspicious swallows were ironic: they haunted Macbeth's castle. My swallows of yesterday were in no such macabre place, but their charm could not hide the hard life which poverty forced on the tiny household whose father has not walked or worked for ten years. And soon the only son is due to be called away for military service.

The villagers have imposed on themselves a stoicism which is not always easy for a foreigner to understand. They seem at times almost insensitive about sickness. There is so little that they can do about it; and they rarely begin to tackle illness before it is too late for them to do anything about it. Yet medicine is a hobby to many of them. Those who can read classical Chinese frequently keep one or two volumes of the classical treatises on medicine and refer to them for the making of simples at home. Those with the modern education of the government schools will have one of the huge modern medical dictionaries, of which there are several in print and which are always readily available for purchase, at a price of several thousand hwan, even in our little village bookshop.

There are two or three Japanese-trained doctors in the area, it is true, but the people seem to have less trust in them than in the drugs they themselves can make or buy. The constant use of medicines of all kinds, especially foreign ones, amounts almost to a passion. Tremendous sums of money are squandered on drugs. Perhaps it is fortunate that the druggists can rarely read the labels on the packets; more stale and useless drugs seem to get sold than powerful and dangerous ones. Yet the regular drugs sought for every kind of illness, from conjunctivitis to high blood pressure, are penicillin, cortisone, and aureomycin. Their high price and effective advertisement must have something to do with it. Even so, they are rarely used alone, especially if the illness is serious: traditional remedies are applied, and the herbalist may be consulted or the 'Chinese doctor' sent for, if not indeed the sorceress. And on every market day the quack is here with his loudspeaker van. It is small wonder that the general attitude to sickness is one more of resignation than of hope, in spite of the addiction to medicines.

Most pathetic are the tragedies that occur in childbirth. In the remoter villages one finds families where there have been eight or nine miscarriages or stillborn children. In one such case among my flock recently, no one thought of sending the mother to the hospital until the ninth child had begun to appear. When one hand had been born and nothing more happened, they decided to take the woman to the hospital. The child, already dead, was removed, and the woman took the racketty journey back to her home, some thirty miles away, by bus the same day. In another case the eighth child of a similar series of difficult births was born in a tiny cottage. The baby lived and was baptized Jude. But the mother died. From then on, the child stood no chance. It was fed on rice water. By the time I was told about it, it was too late for anything to be done: the baby died and was buried without any signs of sorrow or distress. Lack of midwives, long distances from hospitals, bad roads, lack of ambulances or money to pay for them—all these things together with the people's fatalistic lack of preparation for the birth of children combine to make the phrase about 'the danger of childbirth' no empty form of words at the churching of a Korean countrywoman.

The other tragedy we see all too often in our villages is

43

lunacy. In spite of the Korean practice of exogamy among the clans, every community has its half-wits and idiots They are accepted, and even given in marriage. Some people believe that parenthood has a curative effect on the weakminded. Sometimes non-Christians will bring a mentally deficient person along to the church and ask for him to be cured; sometimes doubtless they consult the authorities of the older religions. Lunatics give concern because they create a social problem. At best they are harmless or useless individuals who are a burden on their family's economy. One sees a girl with furtive eyes and a distraught expression lurking around a corner, or a boy with a slobbering mouth and animal habits playing in the yard with a terrible vacancy of thought and lack of control in his movements. Mercifully they seem mostly to die young. I have met few over thirty.

Occasionally they become public nuisances. A short time ago poor Agnes began to go crazy. Every day she grew worse. First her eyes went wild; then her hair fell loose; she lost her shoes and part of her clothes, and no one knew where she slept. She mooned around, Ophelia-like, carrying flowers, singing, screaming with laughter. She climbed trees and fell from the branches without hurting herself. She walked into people's houses and sat down to eat or lay down to sleep. Then she grew troublesome and attacked an old woman with an iron bar. She began lighting fires in odd places. It took two young men to control her strength. Her family were desperate because they had no idea of what to do. At last, for other people's sake, they tied her hands behind her back and tied her by a rope to a beam in an outhouse. They were not unkind to her (though someone did tell me that beating is good for madness), but they were desperate. The sight was pathetic—a Hogarth cartoon come to life.

The skylark and the swallow are here as part of the lovely cycle of the rustic year, but the life of the people is hard and often tragic. Last night as I took a turn outside before going to bed it was a fine balmy evening, but over the fields came the convulsed quadruple throbbing of the sorceress's drum and gong. What sadness did that mean in what family in the valley?

The other evening as I passed by the scene of the accident where the two young labourers were killed and the witches had tried to lay their spirits, I noticed a tiny pile of stones and bits of pine branch had started to grow on the roadside. There must be some passing by who still seek to gain some advantage from showing recognition of the power of the spirits in the place by adding their tribute of stone or twig. It will be interesting to see whether the pile grows.

MAY

梅
雨

ALMOST anywhere in the civilized world there must be the same exhilaration about walking down the village street on a spring morning. Our village is no exception. The young trees are almost in full leaf, giving promise of a shade that will be welcome later on when the midsummer heat is intense. The only flowers to be seen now are some decadent mauve sprays of wisteria, gracefully masking the two or three houses that possess it. There is an air of leisurely work-a-day activity, as though there were plenty to do but no need to get unduly anxious about it. The only loafers these days are the little knot of people waiting at the bus stop.

My normal morning sorties are to either the bank or the post office. Both places are delightful in their informality and have the charm proper to public offices in small communities. If you go after closing time you can sometimes be obliged at the back door; at any time you may be invited behind the counter and detained for as long a chat as you are prepared to give time for.

Both are cement-and-board-built Japanese buildings, rather drably decorated inside with not quite the brightest shades of ivory and olive; but the courtesy and cheerfulness of the clerks make either place good to visit. Both have their walls liberally covered with official slogans, and the bank, which is much bigger than it need be, sports a selection of panels of good calligraphy. Nevertheless they make no pretensions to a level of official dignity which would be meaningless in the village. As a foreigner, I doubtless see them at their best; but in terms of service I find that best very good.

I sometimes wonder whether it would cause any great stir if I walked not only behind the counter at the bank, but actually behind the bars of the cashier's cage. I have seen a customer do so once. Perhaps youthful innocence was his passport, for he was a very small boy depositing a few hwan in his 'Children's Passbook', a pleasant little folder with a gaily illustrated cover. Children can deposit any amount from five hwan upwards but can only withdraw money at school-leaving, or in case of some particular need, such as sickness or difficulty with school fees, and then only with the approval of their headmaster. The system looks excellent.

Like most foreigners who have experience of it, I am still not convinced that the use of a seal instead of a signature on cheques and passbooks is at all a secure one. It seems much easier to forge or steal a seal (and the cost of cutting a seal in the village is as low as a hundred hwan) than it is to forge a signature. However, I admit the advantage to the lazy and the busy. If I do not wish to go down to the bank myself, I can always send my seal by somebody else, and it works just as well.

I am not very assiduous with my newspapers, so I missed the fact that the clocks had been changed for summer time. It was a matter of days before I found out. The church services are timed by the sun anyway, and we tend to catch the bus that comes along nearest to the time that we go for it. Only the bank and the post office have really had their lives affected.

The lack of mechanical timepieces can be irritating. Once when I was visiting a village at a distance, I had finished my business and was itching to leave. I said it was time to go, but my companion, Elijah, who was enjoying his chat, looked out of the door and announced, 'There's plenty of sun left yet;

we've no need to set out for some time,' and then relapsed into the conversation. Korean country life is firmly geared to the cycles of the sun, moon, and stars.

The village sewing school has held its half-yearly graduation ceremony. Such schools are an intriguing feature of rural life. They aim at helping the village maidens to prepare for marriage by perfecting their knowledge of foreign *couture* and embroidery. They also succeed in more or less reproducing the atmosphere of more dignified academic establishments, not least because they give the girls an otherwise inaccessible chance of school comradeship in their middle or late teens, even though it may last only for six months. This one is conducted in our church orphanage by three of the village women. The first thing most of the girls will do on starting at the school is make a blue skirt and white blouse on the normal high-school pattern and thus mark out their status as students. They return to their Korean clothes only after graduation, when they begin to think of getting their hair frizzed and crimped into the horrid messy style which is the local badge of the young married woman.

Their graduation ceremony was short but very, very formal. After the presentation of the certificates and the various speeches of the staff and visitors, we came at last to the farewell speech from the students. It was written in ill-spelled Korean script (most rural writing is extraordinarily ill-spelled) on an apparently endless belt of white paper. As the girl progressed with the reading, tears came nearer and nearer to choking her, but she manfully struggled through to the end, unconscious of the giggles of the few girls who were not leaving the school that day. The proceedings of the morning ended with the graduation song. It is a local composition, and I thought it overlong. It started all right but soon broke out into a sob. A girl turned to hide her face in her companion's shoulder, and the companion broke down at once. Soon only the wheezy harmonium was left struggling bravely with the melody through a pandemonium of wails, second not even to a major funeral.

My first impulse was to laugh; but I saw a man, older than myself, who had walked in, dabbing away at his eyes. It occurred to me that the day did mark a break of great importance in the lives of these girls. For six months they have been excused from housework and have had a life of sewing and games. Within a year many of them can expect to be married off. It is a minor change in the pattern of Korean life, but it still does not obscure the fundamental identity of the villagers' existence with that of their great-grandparents.

Nor does that other new thing in the village, the latest thorn in my side, the innocuous-looking wooden hut topped with a plain cross, where the latest of Korea's quasi-religions has struck a foothold. It has been there only a week or two. It came in with a political flavour for some people, and arouses curiosity mingled with distaste, because the tenets of the sect are well known. Active proselytizing from the established churches, combined with denigration of them, has been started, and every night, well into the night, the sound of hand-clapping and hymn-singing goes far into the hours of darkness. At present the congregation—like that of Jehovah's Witnesses, who got here a few months earlier—is mostly of children.

Not long ago I was reading C. A. Clark's *Religions of Old Korea* and was intrigued by his brief description of a creed called Poch'ŏn-gyo (for which I will hazard the translation 'Doctrine of Universal Heaven'). I was talking about it to one of the village worthies in my room when Michael, the boy who does my cooking, came in, overheard the conversation and made an interesting contribution. He comes from a remote and fairly backward mountainous area near Tangjin, across the gulf to the south. About the time of the outbreak of the Korean War a man came from Kyeryong-san, near Taejŏn, and began to preach Poch'ŏn-gyo in Michael's home village. About twenty-five people were converted, and their practices became well known in the place. They used to foregather every day in a borrowed room and pray together for an hour or two. They made constant repetition of the formula:

T'ae-ŭl ch'ŏnsa, Wŏn'gŏl Hamni, Chuwaduri:
Hŭmch'i Hŭmch'i Saap'aa!

which all the village children got to know. I sometimes still hear Michael chanting it as he works away in the kitchen. (Actually he has it a bit garbled.)

He tells no tales of ecstasy among these people, though they claimed that their true believers could see their ancestors. They had some kind of public confession of sins, and they distributed, by way of propaganda, pieces of coarse Korean paper with impressions of large square seals on them. These talismans were supposed to protect against evil spirits. The leader of the group was a woman who became mad and died of some revolting disease about a year ago, which seems to have damaged the cult's prestige somewhat. Yet it was not only the most ignorant who were adherents because at least one *myŏn* (township) council member was associated.

The sect is a branch of the Hŭmch'i-gyo, founded by Kang Ilsun in the first decade of this century. The word Hŭmch'i is associated with the famous Tibetan invocation 'Om-mani-padmi-hum', usually called 'the Jewel in the Lotus'. I believe there are in Korea some seventy such sects as this. What I have learned suggests that Poch'ŏn-gyo is a syncretistic religion not entirely dissimilar from the better known Ch'ŏndo-gyo, though perhaps appealing to a different class of people. Yet the most interesting reflection of all is that there are points of contact between this cult and the eccentric and more or less ecstatic offshoots of Christianity which have been embarrassing the Korean churches during the past few years. In fact the suspicion is that shamanism is trying to keep itself a niche even within the structure of Korean Christianity.

Spring came and went so quickly that I scarcely noticed it. It seemed to have been washed away in the more than usually persistent rains this year. The swallows are back, and the cuckoo is calling, but I have a feeling that they were here long before I noticed them.

It is hard not to get caught up in the increased expenditure of energy that belongs to the season. The day starts early, when the sun rises, and folk work hard through it, without the siesta that the full heat of summer will force upon them. The result is that most people retire to bed earlier in spring than at any other season, tired out from the willing expenditure of the day's energy.

The countryside has changed again, and is now wearing its green dress. The rain has made the barley shoot up and caused an outbreak of a kind of black mould on the young ears, for which crowds of school children have been sent out to cull the standing grain. In spite of this, a good harvest is expected. The rice has been sown in the seedbeds, which are now all wearing that vivid green peculiar to thickly planted rice seedlings. A few farmers have been able to begin transplanting, but most of the paddies are still in the preparation stage, and even the ploughing is still far from finished.

Irrigation is well under way, and there is plenty of water. The most attractive sight is the tall water wheel worked by a man treading it on the topside—it looks best when silhouetted against the sunset sky. I wonder if its efficiency compares with its attractiveness. Superficially, so many of the Korean methods of lifting water from one level to another look in-efficient, but, whether from necessity or for more positive reasons, they yearly continue in use.

Building and road-mending are springtime activities. I have felt deep satisfaction at seeing work begun on our roads, though it will need much sustained effort to make up for decades of neglect. The *corvée* by which local people work on the highways, each village taking responsibility for a particular stretch, is not a very active system hereabouts. The main road for the village is forty years old, but they still call it the New Road.

Building flourishes better. The village grows in every direction, with granaries, houses, and shops going up. The raising of the central beam is always a great occasion that shows a neat blend of religion and convenience. Large quantities of hot rice-cake thickly coated with red beans are set out, and deep bows are made before the spirit who will dwell in the beam. Then the builders sit down to rest and enjoy the rice cake. All the village children also come out, and go away with their grubby pockets stuffed with the warm sticky cake. It is not much of a ceremony, as ceremonies go. Indeed the most impressive thing is the scuffle as the children crowd round the woman with the cake-boiler like hungry chickens at their trough. Inevitably the feathers fly as two boys get hold of opposite ends of the same big piece.

When the beam is up, the house is ready for its roof, but still has no walls, only a frame of wood, and we have the regular spectacle of the Koreans building from the top downwards. After the roof is on, sorghum stalks are tied in a grid over the wooden frame and then plastered with red mud to make the substance of the walls. The chief expense in building is for wood, roofing, and glass, if any is used for windows. Any and everybody may help in the work, just as in sinking a well. The budget, however, must also make ample allowance for wining the builders and providing plenty of food for the beam-raising.

夏

SUMMER

In huge hat and rice-straw rain-cape,
    shouldering my hoe through the drizzle. . .
Between one plot and the next
    I lie down in the green shade.
A youngster, leading his cow this way,
    stops to rouse me from my sleep . . .

Anonymous

JUNE

麥

秋

WE STARTED our *nanjang* on the Buddha's birthday, the eighth day of the fourth moon. I can think of no better way of translating the word *nanjang* than describing it, but I am tempted by the expression 'kicking up a dust in the market place', which is literally and figuratively an accurate description.

It began with the erection of three tall masts from which floated the red, yellow, and blue streamers that can only announce agricultural dances, and the huge paper carp and lanterns which belong to the Buddhist feast. Then for a week there were special gambling concessions, and the village became a rustic Monte Carlo. Everywhere men were squatting on straw mats, shouting as they threw up the bevelled *yut* sticks or crashed down the Japanese flower cards that correspond to the occidental aces and trumps. There was a kind of fantan, and many variations of games less familiar to me. On the two market-days every gambling mat was the centre of a thick little crowd, but even on the other days, from the early morning onwards, men were playing *yut* in the shade, and the Market Development Committee, functioning for the time being under the traditional name of the 'Old Folks' Aid Society', was receiving dues from the croupiers. The wine-shops, of course, flourished even more than usual. And the fortune-tellers came out, including several depressed women with caged finches which would hop out of their cages and pick up folded billets from a tray for a gift of twenty hwan. Each paper contained the details of the payer's future.

The village was crowded, and as I walked down the street I heard every Korean accent I could recognize, from the far north to the deep south, as well as the many nuances that belong to the various villages in our county. Dust was everywhere, and all the excitement of money changing hands faster than usual.

A twenty-foot-high swing had been set up at one end of the grain market and decorated with pine branches and red bunting. There was to be a competition on it. The first prize was a gold ring, the second a bolt of undyed cotton cloth, the third a half bolt, and the last an aluminium saucepan. Most of the competitors were young men. (I have once again to contradict the old story that only women swing in Korea.) A tall bamboo marked with knots of scarlet bunting was set up beside the swing to judge the height that the swingers reached. Since most of them, with both hands and feet firmly bound to the swing, got the ropes to the horizontal, I was at a loss to understand how the judging could be managed, and I still have not found out.

Even after watching for as much time as I could spare, I found this swinging breath-taking. The clean lines of the taut young body swing rhythmically in arcs increasing until they reach the horizontal stretch of the ropes, when suddenly the rope slackens and bucks slightly before the man falls backward in the reverse arc to return forward with what seems incredible slowness into the same position again. It is obviously an agricultural sport, for men who have an even development of every muscle in their bodies.

Then there was a tightrope walker, but he was a professional and neither brooked nor invited any competition. To the sound of delicate music on bamboo flutes and drums he walked, danced, even jumped a little, and sang old songs on the tightrope, balancing himself with a huge white paper fan. But he was not popular, and on the second day he packed his bags and left—takings were too small. The old men wagged their heads and recalled the days when the tightrope walkers had been pretty boys in long-sleeved Buddhist robes and pointed caps. They did not care for this gentleman with the oiled hair and hussar jacket, who breathed more of the western circus than of the *nanjang* of the days gone by.

Without doubt the most popular thing in the whole festival was the troupe performing farmers' dances, which they did with almost every possible embellishment. They were a prize-winning team belonging to the county, but like the English county cricket teams, they find no necessity to be either natives or residents of the county they represent. They are strictly professionals and still to some extent itinerant.

In comparing them with the villages' own dancing teams, I found that what they made up in showmanship and panache they lacked in simple enthusiasm. When we have a competition between villages there is less bravura but much more fun. These men had always an eye on the money-bag. Furthermore, some of them were rather long in the tooth. However, they gave us a good show, generally twice a day, for a week, alternately in the rice market and the fish market. The genuine pleasure of the villagers in the rapid drumming, the infectious rhythm of the gongs and cymbals, and the fantastic swirling of the swivelled streamers on their hats, was undeniable.

In the mornings the dancing team was available to perform *kosa*, prayers for blessings at the houses or shops of those who required this service. The householder would set up a measure overflowing with hulled rice, with green paper money arranged starwise on the top of it. The money was weighted down with a hank of undyed yarn, whose length symbolizes unlimited good fortune. First the dancing boys would bow to the house, and the dancers would form up and perform a short dance. Then a drummer and a cymbalist would accompany a long and barbaric-sounding prayer. At last the boys would bow again, and the team would collect the money and the yarn, and pour the rice into a bag.

The boys are a very interesting feature of the teams. They are sometimes called *hwadong* (flower boys) and are almost certainly historically connected with the famous Hwarang, the Order of Flower Boys of the Silla dynasty. They wear red skirts with sleeveless, split-skirted blue coats over them. Over the coat is a series of crossed and knotted sashes in blue, yellow, and red. Their heads are done up in red sashes tied into turbans with heavy ruching over the forehead. I am told by the oldsters that this headdress is modern. In days gone by the boys wore long pigtails and looked like girls. Nowadays their skirts are the only suggestion of female impersonation left about them. There were three of them here, about thirteen to fifteen years old. They dance among the men but do not carry tambourines. They wave their arms with the amount of grace you might expect of boys of that age, and they also wave the split skirts of their blue coats. They have a few special dances of their own, but by far their most important function is to dance on the shoulders of the men. When they do this the boys' dancing is of course restricted to movements of the arms, head, and shoulders, while the man below sways rhythmically, moving both arms and legs.

But there is another boy, about nine years old, a little one called *sami*, or monkish child, because he is dressed like a miniature Buddhist monk with a big cornette on his head. He has white cotton sashes tied crosswise round his legs and body, and the man who carries him has him sometimes on his shoulders, sometimes in his hands, sometimes on his head. He throws the child in aerial somersaults and catches him, finally throwing him into the arms of one of the other boys, who is already aloft, and quickly turns the little fellow round, so that now one man dances with two boys overhead. At the climax one of the grown men stands on another's shoulders, and the sami is thrown up to the third storey while two of the other boys are balanced on either side of the men. For a short while one man thus circles the arena carrying four, but it is too hard to last long, and the boys tumble down and run out and press the knees of the spectators, saying, 'What about a tip, uncle?'

The same troupe produced the masked drama and the puppet plays. The mask dance has a simple construction. Two or three characters at a time in huge masks take the arena. There is backchat, adlibbed on a traditional outline, and some slapstick fun. Finally they break into a dance with a musical accompaniment. As each scene of the play comes on, the characters change, but there are never many at a time, and the alternation of patter and dance is constant to the end. I could not follow the story, nor could I persuade anyone to explain it, but the spectators enjoyed it hugely. It was done after dark, by the light of flares, but not much insight was needed to identify the tiger, or the Buddhist monk with the pretty girls, or the kindly man who remonstrated with him. All the masks were made of huge half-gourds with papier-maché features and were garish and grotesque.

The puppet show has much to recall Punch and Judy to mind. It is called *kkoktugaksi*, which might be translated Peg-top Bride. The chief character is a bankrupt landlord named Pak Ch'ŏmji, who wanders fecklessly around the countryside in chambering and wantonness, encountering other characters including dancing girls, a concubine, amorous monks, a man-eating snake, and a rather stupid governor of P'yŏngyang.

There is plenty of music and dancing during the action, and it all begins with a complete procession of the characters. They appear over a sheet rigged about eight feet from the ground, and are manipulated by three men. The appearance of each character is announced by a rapid tapping on the top of the sheet with a fan at the place where the puppet will come up. Exits are mostly achieved by one puppet's head bumping another down below the screen. All the dolls are carved or modelled tops to sticks, but some of them have moving arms.

Most are dressed in cloth, and Pak Ch'ŏmji has a tremendous beard.

There is a helpful character called Hong Tongji, who appears naked and unashamed and is painted red. I wonder if he once stood for the innocent child described as red, because when newborn it is naked. Or whether his name, which is really the title of a minor official, has been punned on to mean Red Friend. He has great strength and solves all Pak's problems. After much horseplay, and backchat with the audience, the governor's mother dies, and the good Hong manages to set right some trouble over the funeral procession. At the end a little temple is erected in her honour by the puppet monks, who lean over the screen and invite the audience to subscribe to the temple if they want male issue. Several onlookers handed up 100-hwan notes.

So, late each night, the puppets were packed away with promises of more snakes and dancing girls on the next evening until at last the whole *nanjang* was over and the players left the village. It had been very rustic, very earthy, very unsophisticated, but I had enjoyed it, the village had enjoyed it, and even the old Confucian scholars reluctantly admitted that they had enjoyed it too. These folk entertainments of Korea are sadly neglected, but they are not yet dead. There is still time for more research into their very hazy history and for making them known to many who have as yet never seen them. Such books as are available attribute to the mask plays a history of a thousand years. They do the same for the puppet shows. It is obvious enough that their origin is Buddhist, though, like other moralities, they have turned into farce and gathered a satiric force, attacking both clergy and gentry.

What is the truth about Korean Buddhism today? Between the Ministry of Education's recent figure of three and a half million Buddhist believers, and the common statement of foreigners that Buddhism is moribund, where lies the truth?

I doubt whether the question is susceptible of an answer that will satisfy the Western observer's desire for measurable fact. Buddhism seems to be sufficiently tolerant, at least in Korea, to live at peace with other religions, even on the same soil. The commonest description of any non-Christian religious practice by unlettered countryfolk is that 'it's Buddhist.' This may be because they know no more dignified word for the complex of practices that stem from animism and shamanism; or it may equally well be due to the fact that Buddhist monks have not always spurned to be employed for shamanistic purposes, just as the sorceresses have sometimes built temples with an obvious architectural debt to Buddhism.

Genuine Buddhism seems to count for very little within the two or three hundred square miles of my parish, although I have found and visited three tiny temples. The most accessible is dedicated to the Buddha known as the Teacher. It is very close to a small village set in a dull piece of relatively flat land, utterly unlike the setting of the great tourist-attracting temples in the mountains. The enclosure is no larger than that of a middling-sized house. It contains the monk's house and the single, undistinguished temple building, which is practically unadorned save for the board over the central door bearing the name of the place. Inside it is clean but not particularly attractive. The three images are of white clay with red and blue on their faces. They are crude and quite small. There are one or two books, published since the Liberation, giving the texts of prayers in parallel columns of Chinese and the Korean transliteration of the Chinese.

The only monk is a married man whose wife is much younger than he is. He is quite deaf, so the visitor's part of the conversation must be carried on with pencil and paper. He earns a living by farming his land, and prays regularly in the temple, but I gather that outsiders come only on the great spring feast of Buddha's birthday. Rather a dull and gloomy little establishment.

He has shown me an interesting document, a book made by a local schoolboy who was living with him a year or two ago. It is a series of water-colour pictures in a style partly indebted to contemporary comic strips, showing all the heavens and hells of Buddhism with artless enthusiasm. A few days later I met the maker of the book, now a university student, on a local bus. I asked him whether he was a Buddhist believer. He said he was not and never had been.

Our second local temple is the Temple of Profound Joy, on the Mountain of Abundant Virtue. This is less accessible, situated among the growing pines on a hillside overlooking the sea. There is a large and respectable hall whose board proclaims the name of the temple. Inside there is a life-size stone image of the Buddha, seated in contemplation. The place is inhabited by an ancient nun. She complains of lack of money, but I have seen the place only in the midst of repairs, which seem to be extensive. Meanwhile the smaller images and many pictures and paper flowers have been transferred to a temporary chapel in a room in her house. I cannot gather that there is any real Buddhist faith centred on the place, but the money for the restoration has come from somewhere. At least the big stone statue is the best work of art in the district. On the hillside, part of the temple, is the usual shrine for the spirit of the mountain, in a tiny kiosk of wattle and daub, but the old god has no tiger in this picture and shows his Buddhist cousinship by the pink lotus in his hand.

The third temple has the finest site of all and is most remote, set near the top of a headland on the coast where there is no approach save a footpath. It is called just the Monastery Temple, but has no monks or nuns. Inside the worship-hall hangs the disintegrating black robe of the last monk. In the very poor house nearby there is a family, presided over by a grandmother, who looks after the place. She generally clutches a Buddhist chaplet. So do the children who tumble about in front of the cottage.

But this temple is the most striking of the three. Its name-board proclaims that it is the hall of the Great Hero, which means that the buddha enthroned there is the historical Indian, Shakyamuni. The inside is like nothing so much as a marquee at a provincial flower show. It is crowded with paper lotus flowers and leaves, their pink and green now just beginning to tarnish and fade into brownish white and watery indigo. There is a complete set of what archaeologists like to call 'cult objects', but the only books are two handwritten volumes of a list of benefactors. Two walls are covered with brightly coloured new paintings of buddhas and others, including the mountain spirit with an altar to himself. (Here he has both tiger and lotus.) In the centre of the altar table is the usual little wooden tablet with the name of the President of the Republic on it, before some most unprepossessing images. Above hangs the national flag, and the right-hand wall is covered with tier upon tier of paper tablets honouring men of the county who fell in the Korean War. Some have a photograph, some spring from a paper half-lotus. They explain the presence of the paintings, dated according to the Buddhist era as having been done about three years ago.

Does this mean that the families of all these men—several hundred in number—are devout Buddhists? They are arranged according to administrative district and parish, and this is to some extent an official war memorial. I can only guess what light it really sheds on the position of Buddhism in this country: outside Christianity, Buddhism alone speaks of a paradise and a way of helping the dead. The mournful old grandmother complains that there are no monks to keep the place up properly. She taps the wooden block and sounds the old brass bell in prayer, though no one comes.

But this is only our district. Near Seoul we can see a newly built Buddhist church, with a blue dome and a swastika in place of a cross. The capital also has a flourishing Buddhist institution in the big Tongguk University. In other places there are signs of a Buddhist young people's society, and I have met intelligent young men who claim to be convinced Buddhists. I have also met many young novices. Two weeks ago I was away from home, in the far south. I walked into the court of a famous and beautiful temple where there are now twenty-five monks. The place was lovely in the twilight, and a soothing drone came from the main hall, where a row of monks stood monotonously invoking Kwanseum, as the Koreans call Kwan-yin, the famous Bodhisattva of Mercy, before the lofty images. The atmosphere was irresistibly like that of a French Cistercian abbey during summer vespers.

A monk came out, probably to relieve the monotony of the unending repetition of five syllables. Attracted by the dark robe of the priest of another faith, he came over to speak. He was a mere boy of seventeen or eighteen. He spoke with an an enchanting southern lilt, with perfect manners and a very select vocabulary. As he spoke, he constantly gestured with his beautiful hands that were tapered like those of the images he served, and enhanced by his flowing grey sleeves. He was zealous and well informed. He had been brought up as a Protestant child in the Holiness Church; but Korean Protestantism has no satisfaction to offer to people of his nature, so he had left his home and the parents who could not understand his attitude to life, and gone into the temple. His parents do not know where he is. I can well understand what had attracted him. I have several such young friends among the monks. They have a free, almost bohemian life, frequently moving from one monastery to another. Sometimes they are well educated, and their education is liberal. I have found an excellent array of reference books in a cell on a mountain peak near Seoul, where I surprised the young religious on a sunny afternoon which he was consecrating to a Hemingway novel.

Of course there are people who make innuendoes about the monks' morals and their laziness. But monks will argue passionately for their creed. And they ache, like all men, for peace. In the great mountain temples they may perhaps sometimes find it. I am reminded of the serene boy who gently drew aside his pale gauze sleeve from the spring when he gave me a cup of cold water from the crystal well at Sudŏk-sa. For here is mysticism, beauty and love, with some measure of self-abandonment. Buddhism is deeply engrained in Korean popular culture, however little the laity may understand it. Yet not all fervent Buddhism is pure: the creed is notorious for its ability to syncretize. This spring I visited a flourishing little temple with six monks. It also included a shrine of the mythical founder of Korea, Tan'gun, and another of the Chinese god of war. The janitor was a keen Jehovah's Witness.

The fifth moon has come, and with it the transplanting of the rice and the swing festival. The flat landscape is daily more thickly dotted with figures as more and more get down to the rice planting—literally down to it, knee deep in cold water and with their backs bent to do a centuries-old job in which there is as yet no satisfactory substitute for a man's fingers, if the ground is to yield its maximum increase. It is hard work, and it gets harder as the sun mounts higher in the sky, but there is an air of festivity about the planters and all the joy of a picnic in their mid-morning break for food by the roadside. The boys trot gaily from seedbed to field with towels tied round their heads and heavy loads of vivid green seedlings on their backs.

Koreans hate to be alone: this week the solitary labourers are few and far between. In the evening the schoolboys roll their thin summer trousers high over their thighs and join the rest of the family in the muddy fields, working till late dusk. By nightfall the steely surface of the fields is spangled with the wispy stars of the well-spaced plants, and most of the roads and paths are scattered with wasted bundles of dropped plants, now past any hope of reviving and bearing grain.

The swing festival is called Tano, the high noon of the year. It is the fifth day of the fifth moon. There is a festival for the first of the first moon (New Year's Day), the third of the third (when the swallows come back), the seventh of the seventh (for relief from the heat), and the ninth of the ninth (when the wild geese arrive and people who know how drink wine infused with chrysanthemum petals). They all reflect the high esteem which the Orient has for odd numbers.

Tano is a great day for sports, especially wrestling but also bullfighting in the south (the bulls fight each other, not men). Many other games and customs are associated with the day, such as the habit of the girls to wash their hair in an infusion of the wild iris root and to dream of sweethearts. But it is pre-eminently the day for swinging. It fell on Sunday this year. A huge swing was hung on pine poles in one of the school-yards. Another was hung from a tall pine tree by the church door. Elsewhere they were suspended from bridges and other suitable points, but it was not only the girls in their bright Sunday best who risked their necks in the exhilarating exercise. Singly or in pairs (paired swinging, two on one swing, is both more dangerous and more exciting because more momentum can be gained), boys and men, as well as women and girls, happily did the right thing on the right day, in spite of the commonly told story that swinging is a sport strictly reserved for the female sex.

The 'barley pass', a friend tells me, is the highest of all the mountains in Korea. I can well believe it, even though the pass exists in time rather than in space. It is the name of the season of food scarcity. During these weeks before the barley ripens, when last year's grain stocks are dwindling, prices soar. My own marketing in the village is not only expensive but also difficult because there is so little that can be bought by way of fresh food. The very *kimch'i*, the indispensable Korean raw vegetable pickle, usually so strong in flavour, seems insipid, and the villagers are complaining that this is the worst season of the year. Food and money are scarcest, flies and mosquitoes are increasing, the heat is getting more trying, and work is gathering momentum.

That increased work in the rice-fields calls for musical accompaniment. Almost every evening from some hamlet or other the sound of the farmers' music will be wafted over the valleys. Sometimes the men will sing together as they work in the paddy, and the pipes and drums will accompany them as they go to and from home, or during their lunchtime intermission. At the side of the field is the tall bamboo pole with a finial tuft of pheasant's feathers and a huge ragged blue pennant covered with Chinese characters. The saucer-shaped hats with swivelled crests and tassels are out again, and the completion of the rice-planting is having its semi-religious celebration of music and dancing. I am told that sacrifices are offered before the pennant poles, but I have not actually seen it being done in this district.

The growing crops have transformed the whole countryside into a patchwork of infinitely graded green and blue. It is easy to understand why Oriental languages are so vague about distinguishing these two colours, and why Korea should also have the name of Ch'ŏnggu—Blue Hills. In the rain-washed air of our cool evenings the misty colour of the distant mountains, the deep shade of the pinewoods, and the lush fresh green of the fruit and oak trees are a comfort to the eyes. In the valleys the crops run from the vivid emerald of the rice shoots, through the dark leaves of the beans and peppers to the bright light blue of the stalks of the standing barley, which is only here and there yet touched with the gold of the ripening grain.

It is a good time for walking among the villages, though a bad time for parochial visiting because the menfolk are so rarely at home by day. Even the post-office clerks go to work in their paddies in the evening, and the casual labour of the village is fully employed—indeed some farmers are bringing in workers from outside. But the sick must be visited, the women always like the priest to call, and some of the new houses have still not been blessed. Two of my recent cases of sickness have been children in households that were only partly Christian. All my efforts and those of my catechists have not persuaded the families to trust the doctors, and the sorcerers have been called in. In one case the sorcerer was a man who did his work in a relatively dignified way, without drums. He claimed that it was the spirit of the house site who was troubled because he had not been properly consulted when the house was enlarged recently. In the other case, in spite of the sorceress's gongs and incantations, the child died. The villagers are not much surprised. The sorceress is fairly new to her job, but she'll do better as she gets into it, they say.

There are other methods of dealing with sickness, however. I was sitting chatting with a couple of oldish Christian men— the sort of countryfolk who still grow the nails of their little fingers long. One of the women suddenly asked the older of the two if he had his needle with him. He hadn't, but the other man had. One of the children had a bad stomach. The man slapped the little pot belly, which looked as if there were nothing further wrong with it than that it had been stuffed with too much rice that morning. He then produced his needle, which was a lusty instrument like a bradawl, cleaned it on the hair of his head, made the sign of the cross, and firmly pricked the fleshy part of the child's hands and feet, once each. The shouts were loud but brief. Conversation was immediately resumed. The theory is akin to that of bloodletting, but this sort of acupuncture does not release much blood. Everyone was sure that the indigestion would be cured by the next day.

Some of these women still maintain the fast-fading custom of displaying pride of family by the colour of their clothes. If their husband is alive, they wear crimson ribbons to tie their bodices. If they have living sons, their sleeves may be edged with blue, the colour of youth; but I know very few hereabouts who commonly wear the blue cuffs. One woman who does keep this custom is about to lose her only son to the army. Three boys will leave the village together. The coming of their call-up notices was sent round the village by the bush telegraph within an hour, and their friends and others came to examine the document and try to understand all the Chinese characters on it. Even those who can read none of it like to handle it. For nothing is really private in our village, and least of all if it has been written down.

A recurring question in letters from friends in England is echoed by the question of foreigners living in Seoul. 'How do the country people accept you?' There are other forms of it, such as 'Can you really work together with Koreans?' 'Can you really establish contact with your flock?' At first the answers seem self-evident, and the questions seem useless; but a little reflection is enough to make me less prepared to give a straight answer to any of them, and the more I think about it, the larger looms one single factor in the situation: the Korean language.

Korean has a reputation for being fantastically difficult for native English speakers. This is undeniable. We have to reverse our thoughts and turn our sentences inside out before we can express them in Korean, because the syntaxes of the two languages are so completely different. Listening is no easier, because Korean threads its sentences together in a way that is fatiguing to the English mind and makes concentration difficult. Naturally there are very few foreigners who are good speakers of Korean, indeed few who are even tolerable. Missionaries are mostly quick to learn enough to get by with in the kitchen, the pulpit, and the classroom, and speak a blatant translationese even in these circumstances. I am still surprised that week after week my parishioners will return to sit at my feet and endure the unnatural phrasing and the irksome foreign accent of my preaching. The fact that they do is some testimony to the absolute value of the Church's message.

There is no doubt that the daunting difficulties of the language have made everybody lower his standards. The foreigner is content with a bad accent and a poor command of Korean, and the Korean is so glad that the foreigner is trying at all that he overpraises where no praise is due. I grow tired of being complimented on speaking good Korean when I have done no more than say good morning—indeed I have received the compliment in a conversation conducted entirely in English. . .

A great source of difficulty is that so few foreigners ever do try to learn Korean. One can understand why they are daunted. The pronunciation offers peculiar obstacles which make it much harder to pick up Korean phrases than, for instance, it is to pick up Japanese phrases. Then the very richness of the language is a difficulty. The talk of the women differs from that of the farmers, and this again from that of the older generation educated in the cottage schools. The newspaper and the modern textbook have an entirely different vocabulary, as slick and sophisticated as the country talk is rustic and salty. It is easy for the foreign student to be competent in only one field or in only one type of conversation.

The rapid development of Korean studies by Korean scholars, and the slow opening of Korean studies in Europe and America will gradually make it easier for us. Yet we shall never be quite free of misunderstandings. A churchwarden sent a boy to buy incense for my church. It was entirely a transaction between Koreans. The next Saturday evening at the altar I found blue flames coming from the thurible, and quite the wrong smell The Korean for incense is *yuhyang;* *yuhwang* is sulphur. It really is a difficult language.

The one Western comfort which I seriously miss in my village is a bath; but six miles away, on the coast, there is a handful of American soldiers, and they have a splendid tiled shower room and lots of hot water. Weather permitting, I have a pleasant evening's walk with an excellent excuse. It seems absurd to go on foot from an out-of-the-way village to an even more remote hamlet in search of the fleshpots of the West. But the bathroom is not all: after the shower I am generally invited to a full-length film show, probably in cinemascope and in colour. Within the little compound, one might as well not be in Korea for all the difference it makes.

Coming out during an interval while they change the rolls of the film, seeing the bay, smooth and calm under the evening sun, hearing the farmers singing over the paddies, I find that the poignant contrast between the real world of the countryside and the unreal world of the film is complicated by the impression of a third plane, the world of these soldiers. It is real enough, but unrelated to the world outside the fence, where the people live frugally, without baths and without films.

Yet it is related a little, because the soldiers employ a large Korean staff. The work is well paid and eagerly sought after. There are people in the neighbourhood who will undertake to introduce intending applicants for a reasonable monetary consideration. I know, because there are some who think that the foreign priest's introduction might be both more effective and more economical. The Americans are not to be blamed for these purely Korean rackets. Nor are they to be blamed because they cannot achieve more than the most superficial intercourse with the local people; but there they are, neighbours who cannot communicate. Of late the whole question has been brought home to me even more forcibly.

An hour and a half away by jeep is one of the larger US bases. It is well outside my parish, but I am the nearest foreign priest, so I have been guineapigging there during the chaplain's absence. Here in a vast and bleak site is a small and purely American town, with that air of insecurity that belongs to non-permanent military establishments. In spite of large numbers of Korean employees and prostitutes, nothing about it suggests Korea. Yet it is an important feature of this piece of countryside and has created on its doorstep a Korean village that lives off its moral and physical refuse.

To the Americans who entertain me after mass I am a novel curiosity, someone from the other side of the barbed wire: in fact a visitor from Korea. I am plied with questions about Korea on every subject from politics through marriage customs to diet. I am asked to check stories about Korea, and fantastic some of them are. It is hard to blame anyone for that. The language barrier seems unsurpassable. The only Koreans the American soldier knows are the pathetic waitresses, the cocky young men with a smattering of bad American who work in the place, and the Cyprians outside the gate. He cannot understand why the first name of so many Koreans should be Lee, as though they were all anti-Yankee. The girls go by Japanese nicknames like 'Skoshi' and 'Josan'.

What does the Korean countryman know of the American? Perhaps even less. He knews that Americans are wealthy and that they bring prostitutes and dope-dealers in their wake, quite apart from various other rackets and opportunities. (At least there is no ill feeling.) To the man with a foot in both worlds the situation is tragic, because it does justice to neither.

So it was some consolation when I returned home on Sunday to find two young American airmen gleefully ransacking my bookcases. Somehow they had crashed the barrier, learned some Korean, and started to talk it. Now they were plunging into Chinese characters, like colts in an apple orchard. Even the pseudo-sophisticated camp employees are secretly moved and pleased; but their own fellows think they are crazy.

This week the barley is ripening well. A good deal of it is already cut and was threshed almost at once. Some of it is threshed by a machine which runs all night long, but much of it is still done by hand. A man slings a short rope round the waist of a sheaf and swings the whole thing in wide circles over his head and right shoulder, bringing it down heavily each time on a wooden mortar laid upon its side. The grain flies in all directions, and a fine pile of needles from the broken beards of the barley collects near the mortar. The work is finished with a wooden flail, an instrument which is easier to control than its old English counterpart because it is jointed with a wooden dowel instead of a thong. The straw is cast aside, reckoned poor stuff by comparison with the more pliable rice straw, and fit only for fuel, manure, and making the straw rain-capes which our farmers still use a good deal.

Almost overnight, it seemed, some of our market prices eased, but we are not quite out of the barley pass: the police notice in the village inn still encourages us to expect barley or sorghum in our cooked rice. We look forward to seeing our bowls sparkling again with the unalloyed white of the best rice, which every Korean believes is his birthright. Some fresh vegetables and fruit (cabbages and cherries) are appearing, but it is hard to be persuaded that price fluctuations are not swayed as much by psychological as by economic considerations.

The farmers are bitterly complaining that they require rain badly so that they can finish transplanting the rice, but they vary in their estimates of how much longer the crop can wait. Farmers are professional complainers, and the non-farmer is puzzled to know exactly how difficult their situation is. However, a few are busy again shifting water from the lower to the higher paddies.

The chief work of the week is weeding. Many are doing this in co-operative bands, and the big banner is still preceding the single file of white-clad labourers (where else in the world do men put on clean white clothes to work in the mud?) from field to field. With them go the wine bottles and a group of boys with scarlet, yellow, and blue bandoliers, dancing with tambourines, swirling the great tassels on their hats like the tails of fly-bedevilled horses. Their charivari is invigorating, but nothing compared to the noise they make while actually hoeing. Fortified with rice spirits, they slash away at the mud between the seedlings, singing wildly and occasionally breaking into a splashing dance, while overhead floats the banner with its paired dragons and the Chinese slogan 'Under Heaven, agriculture is the prime source'—or shall we say, 'Farming is the backbone of the nation'?

I talked to one such band while they were relaxing and drinking among the grave humps beside the rice field. Then as I walked away up the hillside I was followed by a sixteen-year-old boy in grubby hempen clothing who had been helping his father shift water in the paddies. At the top of the hill we sat down to enjoy the splendid view: the island-sprinkled sea on three sides of us; the villages at our feet, half hidden in summer leaves; the graceful form of the Korean-style church on its own hillock; the far blue mountains; and the acres of wooded hills. The rice valleys in this part are small and narrow, but here and there among the trees a hovering cloud of wood smoke betrayed an unseen hamlet cooking its evening meal.

Conversation took a well-worn course, though the boy spoke with a thick rustic brogue. First of all he claimed that the farmers' banner also was connected with the Hwarang, the Flower Boys of the Silla dynasty, a thousand years ago. (He may have been nearer the truth than he knew, for both the Flower Boys and the farmers' band have a religious background.) Did we have such customs in the West? Modern Korea is terribly backward. What did I think was the chief fault of the Koreans? The local headmaster is working very hard to improve the neighbourhood. And what was the chief thing that the West could teach the Koreans? (Apparently the ideals of missionaries are not self-evident.) Then suddenly, what IQ was necessary for an American politician? Such a conversation can be had a thousand times a day (plus a postscript requesting tuition in English) from university freshmen and others in the urban areas. Here it came equally naturally from a boy who lives in a two-roomed cottage, miles from the main roads and the centres of American cultural influence. Having a nest for the house god in the rafters does not stop young Korea from pursuing the comparative study of national intelligence quotients. But then, there is no reason to suppose that by next year my interlocutor may not be a university freshman himself.

Music fills the air all the time now. The noise of fife, drum, and gong comes to my window every evening, and during the daytime I have heard the massed voices of the school children practising the beguiling and plaintive melody of the 25th of June song, in preparation for celebrating the anniversary of the outbreak of the Korean War. It was a beautiful thing if you could not hear the words when the children's inept voices combined with the breezes to blur the martial rhythms into smooth modal curves. On the anniversary day itself the middle-school band joined the performance and ruined the song by asserting its military character. We are proud of this band, sparklingly smart in its black-belted white uniforms with heavy epaulettes and gleaming instruments, but the parade through the village produced no stir save among the urchins, who are home from school this week to help their elders in the fields at the busy season. However, it was only the elders who were in the fields.

I had two foreign guests that morning. 'Why', they said, 'commemorate the outbreak of an unsatisfactory war?' I have lived in Korea just long enough not to have thought of the question myself. The slogans on the banners helped them to understand, but their putting of the question was a pointer to the 38th parallel and the attitude of most of even Korea's best-disposed friends.

In the evening the farmers' music was especially loud and long, part of its exuberance being in honour of the lads who were to leave for the army next morning. During the time since their summonses arrived their friends had been presenting these lads with large banners of white silk mounted on bamboo poles. Each banner congratulated the man, poetically, on 'entering the camp', and some already hailed them (a little prematurely, I feel) as 'Valiant Warrior'. These banners were set up outside the gates of the respective houses. The village presented each recruit with a jade-coloured stole, to be worn crosswise, likewise emblazoned with encouragement. What does it matter that all these customs came from the hated Japanese? At least the honour and glory relieve the gloom of leaving home. One of the boys was a Christian. I gather that there is some local astonishment because he received so many more banners than anybody else. He made excellent use of them by being photographed with the whole collection innumerable times, and with other models varying in dignity from his Sunday school class to his bishop.

At last the morning of departure came. The lorry which took the boys was two hours late. There was a fine drizzle of rain. The village street was a fidgetting forest of white banners. The pipes and gongs and drums were there, escorting the lads in from the hamlets round about. One or two mothers were crying, but it was mostly congratulations and good wishes. Then they were gone, on the back of the lurching truck.

For those with eyes to see, the shadow of the 38th parallel has been a little darker over the village this week. It is not for nothing that in the church I wear a surplice whose tag still bears the name of a martyred priest.

So much summertime conversation seems to be about rain, especially when, as now, there is a lack of it. By proverbial tradition we cannot expect it because the tiny white roses are smothering the briars in the banks and copses, and they say 'it never rains while the wild rose blooms.' What contrast between the meek and modest rose and the lordly spires of the purple paulownia! The paulownia is a fine tree with its broad dark leaves, and now when I see it standing alone in midfield or overhanging a greying thatched roof with its noble blossoms, I can well appreciate that Oriental fancy has given it a mystic dignity, for the divine phoenix will rest on the branches of no other tree. The 'green paulownia', however, to which, strictly speaking, this fancy applies, also brings thoughts of rain, and a sixteenth-century poet wrote one of the most evocative rain poems in the Korean repertoire when he described the raindrops pattering on its elephant-ear leaves.

JULY

霖
熱

ABOUT a week ago the *Korea Times* published a paragraph about old-fashioned schools of Chinese letters in Kangwŏn Province. The general impression was that such schools are fast disappearing, though they linger in remote areas, and that they are anachronistic survivals. My own experience suggests this is a false picture. I have half a dozen of these *kŭlpang* (or *sŏdang*, if you prefer the more learned word) in my parish. I visit them fairly often, and I know there are many others in the central provinces. Furthermore, they still have a useful function in rural society: not many of my villages are out of reach of a *kŭlpang*. Generally each school has about twenty boys. Most of them have finished ordinary elementary school education, but a very few have had no modern schooling at all.

The course still starts with the *Thousand Character Classic* (Ch'ŏnja-mun), also called the *White-headed Classic*. This gives a basic repertoire of classical Chinese characters. The meaning is not studied because the compressed poetic style is too hard for young heads. However, its contents are very similar to those of the next two books, the *Child's Guide to Knowledge* (Tongmong Sŏnsŭp) and the *Primer* (Kyemong-p'yŏn). These two charming little works give the outlines of Chinese philosophy and cosmogony, with glimpses of classical history, a soupçon of poesy, and a first introduction to prose construction. From these a boy graduates to the *Precious*

Mirror of the Pure Heart (Myŏngsim Pogam), a collection of moral aphorisms from China, and the *Universal Mirror* (T'ong'gam), a three-volume ancient history book much esteemed for gaining mastery of syntax. Hereafter he begins the classics proper, working through the *Lesser Learning* (Sohak) and the *Greater Learning* (Taehak) and the *Analects* of Confucius (Nonŏ) to the *Mencius* (Maengja) and the *Doctrine of the Mean* (Chungyong).

Most of my schools have one or two youths who have progressed thus far, but many do not get beyond the first two or three primers. I know one lad of twenty who is working on the *Poetry Classic* (Sigyŏng). For him there remain only the *Book of Documents* (Sŏgyŏng) and the *Book of Changes* (Chuyŏk) which is the zenith of cottage-school studies. These advanced texts are not easy to find these days, but all the books as far as the Mencius can be bought quite cheaply from the travelling book-vendors who come to the village every market day. Some of the cheapest editions are very attractive old-fashioned chapbooks, the last relics of what might be called the folk-printing of Korea. Even so, most of the schools have a good many home-made transcripts lying around.

A visit to any of them is always a pleasure. The boys' faces brighten at the prospect of a chance to relax. The chequer-board or the *paduk* table may come out. (*Paduk* is a game for gentlemen only.) Conversation inevitably includes a few wise saws about diligent study and the discussion of some passage of Chinese. Perhaps one has been able to bring a message in verse from a scholar in another village. Then all can enjoy the exercise of construing it in Korean and appraising the writer's brushmanship: whether his ability in writing Chinese characters is above the normal and has the elegance of real refinement. In summer the doors will be open, and the scent of flowers and the songs of birds and insects will come in from the sunlit garden. So will the flies. In winter the warm floor is cozy and the room smells comfortably of the stored grain and fermenting soya beans. The walls are covered with graffiti: the teacher's proverbs and quotations and the more naive efforts of the pupils. One school now has a blackboard. There are piles of newspaper used for writing practice, and ink splashes everywhere, even on the ceiling. The tables are tiny, and the inkstones are deeply pitted from much grinding of the cakes of black Chinese ink by eager young wrists.

No two schools are quite the same. Foolish Cottage (I use the teacher's literary name) is a much-travelled man, but not very old. Over his cottage door is a bundle of paper and rag clippings as a nest for the household god, while many of his wall inscriptions reflect an interest in Buddhist philosophy. Rustic Chronicler is ancient and toothless and nearly unintelligible, but Reverent Cottage is dapper and bearded. He is a herbalist, and his ceiling is covered with paper bags full of fragrant remedies. He also sports a large cabinet of tiny drawers whose variously scented contents the boys sample in his absence.

Everywhere one has the impression of being among good people, contentedly doing a good work. Is it all useless and unthaic? I am sure it is not. For one thing, the *kŭlpang* has adapted itself to the needs of the village in various ways—not least in that it may have a few girl students. Perfect memorization of all texts is no longer demanded; it is enough these days to read with understanding. But the method of learning is the same as it always was. The boys sit on the floor, generally facing the walls, and recite their texts aloud in a vigorous chant, swaying their bodies from the hips. Since they are all reading different books, the din is tremendous. They take a rest every twenty minutes or so. From time to time the teacher gives explanations or hears repetitions or corrects writing. Formerly there were no holidays at all. Nowadays most of the schools take every tenth day off, to coincide with the local market. (In the smaller places this is held once in ten days, in the larger villages once in five.) Many schools close down altogether during the heavy work season of summer and autumn.

Fees are said to have gone down. They are still rendered in grain. Some teachers demand one bag of barley and two bags of rice for the year, but only ten *mal* of rice, or a hundred *kŭn* (about 132 lbs) of rice and fifty *kŭn* (about 66 lbs) of barley is more normal. The old system of frequent presents of wine and tobacco to the teacher has largely dropped out, but in some schools the custom persists whereby when a boy completes the study of a book he brings rice-cakes to share with the others, together with wine and a gift of clothing for the teacher. School picnics are also not unknown, where the boys may show off their ability to parents and friends.

It is all very charming, very rustic, terribly unprogressive; but it will be a great pity when the last *kŭlpang* finally closes down, and the boys no longer set off after breakfast with a lunch bundle, to chant the classics until sundown. The fact that they are learning Chinese characters is of secondary importance. They are in touch with the only source of sound moral teaching in the countryside today outside the Christian churches, whose moral teaching is all too often deficient. Certainly the regular schools with their distracted curriculum are giving no moral training worth speaking of. The traditional *kŭlpang* education alone can no longer equip a man for public service, but I have seen nothing more cheering in a country school than a lad called Kwanggyu. For months he worked in the morally vicious atmosphere of a large American air base. I first met him as he walked across the valley to school with a Mencius in his hand. The other day I saw him again, planting rice. Mencius may give him chance to weigh the merits of his peasant life against the meretricious allurements of the foreign camp. He, and millions of others, must go on as farmers. It is good for them to have something more than a diluted Western education.

This monsoon weather is depressing. Lowering skies and

heavy damp air sap everybody's energy. Life loses much of its sparkle. Yet there is a certain exhilaration in the periods immediately after the showers: the atmosphere is drenched, but cleansed, and everybody goes outside to enjoy it.

It is so wet that the best thing to do is to get wetter. Most of the village boys have become amphibious for the time being. The channels in the rice fields are swirling with torrents of yellow water full of little fish. You have only to hold a sieve under the cascade at the edge of terrace or ditch, and you can catch your breakfast without effort. There is no point in undressing to get into the water because you're wet through anyway, but of course if a boy is going into the water for pleasure only, he strips for the exercise. We have no appreciable streams for bathing in our area, so the children are making full use of the swollen ponds and ditches. I am sorry for the girls. Though modesty in the Korean village is never false, it deprives the girls of the pleasures of splashing and swimming. Yet there are probably few of them who would enjoy bathing in brooks even if they were brash enough to undress out of doors.

There is no doubt about the exhilaration in the vegetable world. Every tree and plant has increased by inches, and the conifers are showing vivid fresh tips. The path behind the police station, by the shed where the 'Band of the Valiant and Righteous'—that is, the Volunteers—keep their mobile fire pump, has taken on the air of a tropical jungle. The maize and sorghum, which were transplanted three weeks ago, are already taller than a man, and their smooth broad leaves glisten with the moisture that drops from the greenery on every side. Here and there in a dooryard a pomegranate bush is exploding in flashes of scarlet blossom, and the pink and purple hibiscus is vying with the giant morning-glory.

We are just entering the dog days, though there is not now much eating of dogs in this area. Judging from the cartloads of fat puppies I saw in Seoul not long ago, dog flesh is more popular in the city, especially at this time of year. In the country we know the dog days as the time of greatest heat, and the first, middle, and last dog days become a subsidiary way of fixing the date. Nor have we forgotten that the days, like the years, are numbered by the sixtyfold cycle of characters, so that every day also has a presiding zodiacal animal. We expect pig days to be overcast and dragon days to be rainy or at least cloudy. The eighth day of the moon is also noted for poor weather. Luckily the system doesn't claim to be very exact, though it would be interesting to compare its accuracy with that of the scientific forecasts.

I had this information from a man who is expert in the matter of spotting lucky days and knows most of the soothsayer's skill, being able to deal with the sixty-four diagrams, the Dragon Horse of the Yellow River, and the Mystic Tortoise of the Lo River, not to mention the table of nine colours (black, purple, emerald, vermilion, yellow, sea-green, and three whites), and various other occult devices depending on a knowledge of Chinese characters, astrology, and divination. Most of these methods are related to the eight diagrams of the *Book of Changes* (said to be the oldest book in the world and known in Korea as Chuyŏk), but the two books most used now are the *Compendium of Providence* (Ch'ŏn'gi Taeyo) and the *Secret of T'ojŏng* (T'ojŏng Pigyŏl). The first contains almost all the above tables, as well as many other data that the soothsayer requires, and is a difficult work to master. The second is largely composed of a series of mystic Chinese couplets which need interpretation as well as translation. An abbreviation of it, together with a series of letter-writing models, forms the major part of most cheap modern Korean home encyclopaedias.

I was recently out with a young Korean soldier—not a Christian—who consulted such a soothsayer. He wanted to know how this year would turn out for him. Perhaps it was unfair of me to have muddled the old man by reminding him of summer time and Greenwich mean time when we got down to deciding the hour of the soldier's birth, but there was much chewing of pencil butt and consulting of complicated tables before we discovered the two characters which finally showed which set of Chinese verses in the second book held the right answer. There were four couplets, one for each season of the year. I could not make much of them or their interpretation. I gathered that in the spring a fish would make its way from a well to the ocean, which indicated some sort of success. In the autumn my friend's female relations were liable to be troublesome. This all seemed an eminently reasonable forecast.

'But,' said the youth, 'when shall I be discharged from the army?'

'I can't tell you that,' grinned the old man. 'That's much oo difficult. It's not in my books.'

I have recently been turning over some old *Transactions of the Korea Branch of the Royal Asiatic Society*, and found a paper I had never read before on an aspect of Korean rural life of which I must confess more ignorance than knowledge. The paper in question is called the 'Village Guilds of Old Korea' and consists chiefly of data about *kye* collected by Mr. Philip Gillett round about 1912.

Any foreigner who even begins to think of himself as an old Korea hand is liable to smile at the very sound of the word *kye*. (Though more probably he will spell it, as Mr Gillett does, *kae*.) The joke, I think, depends on the despair of those who know the ruinous potentalities of the commonest form of *kye*, the kind which is a hopeful get-rich-quick money club. As far back as the last century, that doughty traveller, Mrs Bishop, noted this kind as being one among the curses of

Korea. Mostly it is dominated, even inspired, by women. A group of them agree to provide contributions to what is in effect the capital of a trading venture. There seem to be various patterns of organization, but they all depend on the success of the trading and the availability of cash on the proper day for the payout. Like so many small trading efforts, they are often entered into with more enthusiasm and confidence than is warranted by the business experience and acumen of the players. The result is frequently a catastrophe and means debts. Korean country folk are chronically debt-prone, but debts incurred by *kye* failures seem to be the most horrific of all. Doubtless there are plenty of successful ones which we foreigners never hear of, because there is no end to the making of *kye*. I know of one woman who regularly travelled from the far end of the country to supervise a *kye* which she had established in my village. It seems to have come to an end, though I have not heard why.

There is a closely related kind of *kye*, which is simply a homespun form of savings bank. A group of people agree each to pay a stated sum (probably a major part of their earnings) to one of their number. The process is repeated at regular intervals, each participant becoming the recipient in turn, until everyone has once received the joint contributions of all the others. No one gains, and no one loses. It is merely a device for getting a larger sum of money than one usually ever has at any given time. Clearly it would be better to save the money in the bank, where there would be the advantage of gaining interest; but these simple *kye* flourish abundantly.

However, it is a mistake to think of *kye* as being exclusively concerned with money. As Mr Gillett pointed out, they had many other objects, from the provision of unofficial police and fire-prevention services, through various kinds of mutual assistance and insurance, to the labour guilds, the burial clubs, and even clan or family unions. The *wich'in kye* is best known. It is a club for mutual help in the case of the death of a parent. There is often another *kye* for the upkeep of the village bier. The bier is dismantled and kept usually in a long, low thatched shed, far out of the village, traditionally eschewed by thieves and children and most others, and therefore a favourite hiding place of lepers. The clubs that care for these things are essential for the villagers' efforts to meet their occasional but crippling funeral expenses.

Not only funerals are expensive. It is no uncommon thing to find a village house containing a huge pan of sprouting beans, which turns out to be the household's contribution to the wedding *kye*. In my experience it is the better-class family in the smaller village that organizes this sort of thing, and contributions are mostly in kind rather than in cash. Of the other *kye* I can write nothing from experience. I know that there are *kye* for the alumni of country schools and that these tend to belong to the group of clubs whose chief object is an occasional—and probably noisy—picnic or party.

Mr Gillett's *kye* were mostly of a different sort, the Taedong Kye and the Ijung Kye (both names imply an organization of the whole village, and were commonly used), which were the old time villagers' answers to the inefficiency of the government in what would now be called 'the lower echelons'. They combined mutual insurance and mutual protection in a system within the national government system. They appointed their own officials, imposed their own fines and penances. Many of their items have a modern ring. They undertook to protect the pine trees from greedy fuel-cutting; they managed 'contributions' to visiting officials (but they also organized resistance to officials whose rapacity passed beyond the bounds of decency). They had election troubles just as we do today—villagers dislike taking on local government responsibility which too often means taking all the kicks and getting no co-operation. They arranged the annual sacrifices at the village shrine. Some of these essentially democratic *kye* still exist, but most have merely transferred some of their characteristics to the modern system of administration, where the old men still make the young men accept distasteful responsibilities.

This weather, changing every other day, shows our country-side under opposite aspects. On the rainy days the rice-fields and the sky both have the same grey-green colour. The farmers in their thatched straw rain-capes look like grotesque tortoises standing on their hind feet, and the whole scene with its misty mountain background reminds me of cheerless early nine-teenth-century engravings in books about China. Then the rare Korean lightning crackles through the sky to illuminate some bedraggled cattle by a dyke, and instead we have a vision of Cuyp or van Ruysdael. The other days are those when the cicada sings as well as the frogs, and the sunlight dapples the paths with the shadows of leaves. These are the days to survey the district from the hilltops and enjoy the sight of the inlets of the sea at low tide, covered with the red edible weed called *namunjae*, great Roman purple tongues of land licking into the fresh green of the paddies. Here and there a vast heronry caps the trees with white, like snow at midsummer. Korea never looks more beautiful, even in the much-vaunted autumn.

The children are having a wonderful time with the season's baby animals. There is a constant audience for a litter of pup-pies under my window; within view and earshot are rabbits and goslings and more puppies; but the boys pay most atten-tion to the fledgling blue magpies. These noisy chatterers are caught with bare hands. They frequently escape and are either recaught or replaced by new specimens. They are very resilient in captivity, and the boys prize them highly because 'this sort don't die.'

The vigour of the co-operative bands of rice cultivators has much declined, though the banner and the band have been out again this week for more weeding. The banner that lives nearest to me bears the legend 'The Divine Husbandman bequeathed us this skill.' It is interesting to see it starting off in the cold light of morning, carried sedately, followed by two or three youths, gyrating perfunctorily.

By contrast, at the return in the evening, when all are well loaded with wine, the banner itself is dancing, and the six youths are whirling like dervishes. The coryphaeus is doing wonders with the peculiarly shaped and rigid-stemmed tassel on his hat, controlling the dancers with an ear-shattering pan of a gong. Outside the house of the headman, where the banner and instruments are kept, there is a prolonged display. The dances are simple. The lads with the whirling plumes and tambourines form one team and the band the other. There are movements of advance and retreat and a circling of the dancers by the band which is like a burlesque of the waltz at the end of *Les Sylphides*.

The energy used in the dusk here by men returning from a hard day's work is prodigious. One would think it impossible without wine. It is also amusing, and the onlookers often laugh. Our side drummer is a little old man with one short leg, and his antics are delicious. The din is exciting, and excruciating.

Some of the villagers tell me in pride that this is 'Korean custom'. None of them knows what it means. Few of them have any idea of who was the Divine Husbandman, the legendary emperor who supposedly taught the Chinese agriculture a thousand years before Tan'gun was born, and three thousand before Christ. Nobody recognizes the twenty-foot tufted pole for the primitive fertility symbol that it is (or are the antics of its bearer at the latter end of the day less ingenuous than they appear?), and nobody notices that the dancing youths are clad in the Five Primary Colours, which have a cosmic significance. In fact, conscious appreciation of the fertility magic is as lacking as it is in its English counterparts, the maypole and the white-clad morris dancers.

What will happen to these customs? They seem strong enough here in Anjung but nevertheless are said to be fading.

Will they be reduced, like their English counterparts again, to tourist attractions and curiosities for folklorists to collect and preserve artificially? Doubtless, like much else of the culture of old Korea, they are bound to sink further into the subconscious mind of the nation. As they pass away there will be a sentimental pang; yet artificial efforts to restore culture are as disastrous as artificial efforts to change it. Both are liable to be more concerned with activities in themselves than with their compelling forces. This is why even the least romantic of us foreigners are saddened when young Koreans are so immoderately keen on adopting the habits and customs of the Western nations, whose religious and social mainsprings of action the Korean does not share and rarely understands. This is why we regret that the education of the country must be so closely patterned on Western models.

My young Korean friend, especially if he is a superior-minded Christian, laughs at the whole idea of Yang and Yin. He is quite unaware of the correspondence between the fundamentals of this philosophy and the logic of Aristotle, or the depth psychology of Jung. It never occurs to him that in his church the men sit on the south, right-hand, sunny side—correctly Yang—while the women are on the shady left-hand north side—properly Yin. He prattles of the spectrum but cannot say what are the Five Colours. Yet in Western literature and the liturgy of the Western church these same five colours have the same evocative values that they have in Oriental tradition, saving only that the regal and propitiatory yellow of the East is replaced in the West by its complementary purple. No, for him it is all existentialism and nuclear energy, Comte, J. S. Mill, and technical progress. It may be right that it should be so. Yet, if man survives the last fallout of radio-active dust and loses his control of technics and statistics, his heart will continue to respond to the symbolism of colours and sunlight; and the ever-repeated cycles of death and resurrection will be his practical experience of the transcendent reality which interests him above all things. A nation's myths do not readily die so long as the nation lives. Perhaps after all, America is Korea's best mentor, for America is a nation without a mythology, least likely to infect another nation's heritage.

The parish priest of Suwŏn is a soul-mate of mine, and I often go to spend a night with him, to relax with an evening of English chatter over a bottle of the local clear wine. Suwŏn is also attractive as our nearest big city and the historical focus of the northern half of my parish. Yet little that you can see in Suwŏn is really very old. Practically everything dates back to one fact: King Chŏngjo's obsession with honouring the shade of his murdered father, the famous 'Coffin King', Chang-jo. This reached its peak when Chŏngjo determined to transfer the capital from Seoul to Suwŏn so that he could be near to his father's grave. That was only 160 years ago.

Some places have an uncanny effect by which they seem to transpire intimations of their history, and this is true of Suwŏn. It was a planned capital which never received its court, a garden of pleasances which were barely patronized; and the destruction brought by the Korean War has increased the sadness of the place. You can feel this sadness most obviously by climbing P'altal Mountain on a summer evening. P'altal is the great hill at whose eastern foot the city lies. You walk up by the crumbling wall, through the myriad trickling streams that burst out in tiny springs all over the hillside, past collapsed bastions and broken arches to the lookout post at the summit. You may regret that the wall is still being used as a quarry by the townspeople, but at the top you will find some weed-covered terraces and the stone bases of what was once a fine pavilion whose view took in all the approaches to the city. Now it is *domus desolata*, and the desolation is not mitigated by the sound of the drums of the dancing school or the vulgar noises of the city with its corrugated iron roofs.

From here you can see all that remains of Chŏngjo's efforts

91

to build an elegant capital. The Great South Gate .s biggest and best, of more beautiful proportions than the South Gate of Seoul, and now the sole survivor of three originals. The Emerald Dragon Gate to the east and the Gate of Everlasting Peace on the road to Seoul (its name, Changan, refers to the ancient Chinese capital) lost their wooden pavilions during the Korean War and are now decrepit massive arches, more dangerous than beautiful. But the little West Gate still stands complete with its semi-circular baffle-wall and the tower for archers beside it, a picturesque reminder of how men could defend themselves against aggressors not so very long ago. Its very smallness adds to its attraction; it is complete—on one side it is even still joined to its wall.

The wall took nearly three years to build and was created for the new capital. Its architect was the famous Chŏng Tasan, who was suspected of unorthodox ideas and liberal notions. Some of these he is said to have introduced, with revolutionary effect, into the planning of Suwŏn's fortifications, whose construction is in turn said to have been unlike previous Chinese and Korean works but to have owed much to ideas derived from Europe through the translations of Jesuit missionaries in China. To the naked eye of the untrained observer nothing of this is at all obvious.

More obvious is the charm of the Water Gate, where the Stream of Refulgent Doctrine tumbles through seven arches beneath the drooping willows, and the Arbour for Viewing the Flowers and Willows (the name is a quotation from a Chinese poem, for Chŏngjo was a literary king) overlooks the Dragon Pool, now a fraction of its former size, outside the city wall. This is a very pretty place, so pretty that one wonders that the city fathers could ever have allowed it to be ruined by the e-rection of a futuristic war memorial nearby. That obscene piece is no credit to anyone. Further along the wall are the remnants of Chŏngjo's drilling ground. with another fine pavilion set above the two broad terraces, now overgrown with weeds, where the garrison was trained.

From the mountain top all these things still hint at the glory which never quite was, for Suwŏn never became the capital of Korea. Its pleasure haunts were never used as much as had been intended. For all that, it was known as Hwasŏng, the Flower City. It was also called Susŏng, the City of Trees, because a large part of the area within the walls remained covered with pines until the Japanese War; or the City of Streams, because it is still full of them. In fact the more prosaic name of Suwŏn, Watery Field, the one preferred by the Japanese administration, is an accurate name for the place. Water lies near the surface everywhere, and there are still rice fields within the walls.

Suwŏn does have some history apart from not quite becoming the capital. It had long been one of the five citadels guarding the approaches to Seoul. (The others were Kanghwa, Kaesŏng, Ch'unch'ŏn, and Namhan Fortress.) From the top of P'altal Mountain one can guess why Suwŏn was strategic. Most of the hills here run in north-to-south ranges. One valley leads down to Anjung. Just north of the city is a conveniently defensible pass in a transverse range, while to the south spreads a flat plain. It was the southern approach which Suwŏn had to defend, so here it is, with hills on three sides and its defences pointing south; and it has convenient communication routes with Kanghwa (through Inch'ŏn) and Namhan Fortress on the west and the east.

On the west, the side of our mountain away from the royal city, is the newer part of the town. The Japanese managed to build the railway from Seoul to Pusan so that it should give the least possible advantage to existing Korean cities. At Suwŏn they temporized by building the station far enough from the town for a substantial Japanese town to grow up along the long road from the station to the city gate. This has neither divided the city nor shifted it, because the main Seoul to Pusan road keeps the centre of the city very much alive.

Chŏngjo's proposed new capital was to have been watered from four reservoirs. Two are left, the West Lake by the railway, and the North Lake by the road. Both were made quite simply by building a dyke across the southern end of a wide, shallow valley. Now they are useful for irrigation, and the West Lake, with its royal pavilion and the trees on its banks, is a great place for fishing and swimming.

This agricultural bent is typical of Suwŏn, a city with a decidedly rustic flavour. Of an evening you can frequently hear the farmers' music of pipe and drum in the heart of the town. In fact this sound is delusory: it means that one of the all-female opera groups is playing at one of the cinemas, and you are being encouraged to go and sit in the fan-fluttering congregation and see a melodrama, in both senses of the word. If you like bright colours and oriental music, it's excellent; but you must also be amenable to gruff-voiced women with huge false beards. Cinemas may not actually be quite so important in the life of Suwŏn as they appear, because they assault the ear with their loudspeakers and the eye with their posters, all the day long. When they do not have live shows, they are showing their pictures most of the day. You can choose between an American western, a Korean film called *Flowers of Hell* (the publicity shows a man and woman rolling in the mud), or films still playing in Seoul's premier houses.

After the cinemas, airmen are most the typical feature of Suwŏn's streets. They too can be seen all day long, having come in from the air base. Like the jet planes that roar overhead and the loudspeakers that blare over the city at most hours of the day, they remind one forcibly of the difference between Korea today and what it was when the walls and pavilions were built. So do the little panders who greet you as you leave the station after alighting from a late evening train.

Yet in spite of the picturesque remains, and in spite of the aggressively contemporary aspects of Suwŏn life, it is the urbane culture that this city nourishes that delights us most.

In the dilapidated Palace of Resplendent Peace, where the great king's portrait once hung, and the court that was once carpeted with tiny white peonies is now rank with weeds, I found boys practising the art of unarmed combat called *tangsu* and girls learning classical dancing; in a summer house in a walled garden I found a group of people meeting to sing old court songs together; and I visited a doctor who plays ancient instruments as well as practising modern medicine.

I like Suwŏn. It would be pleasant to live there.

秋

AUTUMN

Are the chestnuts falling
*   in the vale of russet jujubes?*
The crabs are already crawling
*   in the rice stubble.*
Let's go and buy a sieve to strain new wine
*   and drink with all these good things.*

Hwang Hŭi(1363–1452)

AUGUST

老
炎

ACCORDING to the Korean calendar, autumn is setting in. There are indeed a few signs of its approach: a slight rustiness about the foliage of one or two big trees, a brownish tinge discolouring the surface of the rice fields, where the first ears of grain have already formed. But this is really full summer, and a glorious time it is.

No day begins better than those mornings when I stand at the altar with fresh sunlight streaming through the east window and pitch my voice in the prayers of the mass against the deafening aubade of the birds. In the nearby farmyards the pigs are resuming their never-ending conversation of impertinent or outraged queries and contented chuckles, while the cock is noisily lording it over his hens. The heat increases as the sun rises in the sky. The children are all home from school, enjoying their summer holiday. Their elders too have some relaxation now, a respite during the hottest weather between the heavy work periods of the recently finished weeding of the rice and its harvesting later on.

This is the weather that is called Blazing Heaven: it is not a time for hard labour. Any or all members of a family may spend the greater part of the day in the booths made of straw matting, raised on four poles, which have appeared in most of the dry fields. Here indeed is Isaiah's 'lodge in a garden of cucumbers', because the children who lie on their stomachs chewing grass or who sleep through the noontide up there in the shade of the matting are supposed to be guarding the melons and cucumbers that grow in the fields around

Nothing is more appropriate in this blissful weather than to stretch out and doze. Bernadette, my little black-and-white cat, flakes out in the shade and scarcely stirs all day except for an occasional drink of water. She finds it exhausting even to be stroked. The dogs lie in corners of the yard, with one eye half open and one ear cocked, hating to move but anxious lest they should be trodden on or disturbed by the children.

On market days the heat slows down the pace of trade, and brisk movement in the village, anywhere save down the main street, is hampered by the low awnings stretched over all the alleyways. Some of the older men are wearing vests and cuffs of wickerwork—made from wisteria vines—under their white jackets to keep their clothes from sticking to the skin. Fans are fluttering everywhere. Villagers returning home from market, wearing two or three new straw hats, one atop the other, all carry a new spatulate fan made of yellow varnished paper. Even I find the gentle fan a great comfort in church when the rubrics would have me sit and swelter in a cope, or to keep my hands busy during the sermon.

There is plenty of fruit to be had: plums, apples, pears, grapes, tomatoes, melons, all in colourful profusion, but only the peaches are really tasty enough to be eaten uncooked. (Quite apart from their widespread bad habit of picking unripe fruit, Koreans do not seem to appreciate good flavour in fruit so much as Europeans do.)

The hibiscus flower is flourishing in every shade of mauve and pink, and sometimes even in pure white, but always with its crimson-purple centre *taché de sang*. The biggest bushes grow outside the police stations and the local government offices: it is a worthy national flower. The gourd vines cover every bank and pigsty, and a good many houses, with big floppy orange flowers; while between the plots of soya beans the beds of domesticated sesame raise chimes of palest mauve bell-shaped flowers. The scarlet peppers are ripening. The cicada sings all day, making a noise like a monstrous clockwork toy.

By force of contrast, the best time of day is the cool of the evening, when Bernadette sneaks out to use the day's stored-up energy in the pursuit of moths and mice. The chickens are jostling for position in their roosting places. A cricket sings in his spiral cage of delicately twisted straw, hanging from the ceiling behind us as we sit on the verandah edge. Fireflies flicker between the branches like midget lanterns, swift and hallucinatory. The stars come out in a deep blue sky, and the moon rises. People sit out late on nights like these. The moon is sentimental and awakens thoughts of home.

Yes, I enjoy high summer in the village; but the calendar insists that Autumn Begins (Ipch'u), and there is no doubt about what the swallows are doing in their daily gathering on the telegraph wires. They are discussing their plans for going south with this Blazing Heaven.

The villagers don't often talk to me about sex. I don't think they talk about it very much among themselves. True, you may occasionally hear schoolboys on the bus discussing their personal development, but by and large sex is an accepted fact rather than a topic for conversation. As one man put it to me, in a Chinese phrase, there are three things necessary for everyone: food, sleep, and sex. In the highly communal life of the village family, where there is no such thing as a private room, children grow up with a natural consciousness of sex, and I doubt whether any Korean father has ever quailed before the ordeal of explaining the facts of life to his son. Small children show their awareness of the basic facts by their unashamed remarks about the behaviour of animals. Some writers about Korea have probably overstressed the puritanical attitude of the people on this subject. Rather is it an unconcerned and naturalistic attitude.

In the old days boys were married off young, sometimes even before puberty. When their need for sexual outlet matured they had no premarital or extramarital temptations. This is no longer true. Many do not marry until they return from the army, where more than a few receive sexual baptism. That experience aside, the occasional lapse is readily pardoned if no scandal arises; but should a child be conceived between an unmarried couple, public opinion—and the girl's parents—will demand that its parents should wed. Indeed, this is one way for young people, if they have the opportunity, to try to force their parents' hands in the matter of spouse-choosing.

I do not think that the old English custom of ascertaining that a woman can conceive children before committing yourself to marry her obtains here. Something very nearly like it does in the connivance at a betrothed couple sleeping together as often as they care to. There is a theoretical disapproval of this, but I know of one case now which is an open secret, and no one is disturbed or shocked. A Korean betrothal is almost as irrevocable as the marriage itself, so there is nothing wanton about such behaviour in the eyes of the village.

Prostitution and seduction are different matters. There are two very rustic-type *kisaeng* called 'bar girls' in one of the village eating-houses. People talk about them, but they hardly make a gay-house, and nobody identifies the customers. Maybe the itinerant merchants who come on market days and stay overnight? I don't know. But there are few or no secrets in a Korean village. Liaisons there may be, not talked about, but certainly not secret. Young widows have a traditionally bad reputation. On the other hand I know a girl whose husband is in the army and who lives alone and shares a room with her brother-in-law. I am told it is all right because they are members of the same family.

Late one night last winter I was walking back over the

frozen fields with a young schoolteacher, returning from an emergency sick call. As we entered the village a naked girl in her late teens came whimpering up to us. We asked where her clothes were, and she led us by devious back alleyways to a house on the far side of the village, where her clothes were piled on the verandah. It was a shabby one-room cottage. The rough fellow who lived alone there told us she had stripped in his room and broken a big jar. He showed us the pieces. She claimed he had attacked her. No one thought much of the man, but the girl had a reputation as a simpleton. The story seemed fairly clear to me. I should think our village is reasonably chaste, but none of its inhabitants are angels.

There is no known case of a concubine, but conversation about people reputed to be concubines' sons shows that concubines would be frowned upon in our society.

Educated Koreans often claim that homosexuality is unknown here, in spite of the passionate intensity of many adolescent friendships. But the attitude on this subject too is ambivalent. One of the severest judgements made by the strict Confucian historians against the later kings of the Koryŏ dynasty was a condemnation of their indulgence in the 'love of dragon and sunshine'. (That is the literal translation of the phrase, indicating two male concepts, but it really refers to the name of a classic Chinese royal favourite.) For centuries the gentleman's ideal has restricted sex to marriage and procreation, but there are signs that in rural society paederasty was tolerated if not actually approved. Not long ago I was sitting in the tiring-room of one of my smaller churches, chatting with the churchwarden while the supper was being prepared. There was a lull in the conversation, and then he chuckled and said: 'You know, I never realized paederasty was a sin till I read the Epistle to the Romans.' After hearing the rest of his chatter I was left wondering to myself just what memories lay behind his chuckle.

He said that when he was a boy, only forty years ago, there

103

were often 'pretty boys' in a village. They were especially the favourites of young widowers and sometimes of older and richer men. The boy would receive nice clothes and would be fairly conspicuous, but his position would involve no ostracism and would not impair his chances of marriage. Among the itinerant players, however—the dancers and acrobats and puppet-show people—paederasty, male prostitution, and regular homosexual marriages, sometimes with transvestitism, were common and well known (just as formal tribadistic unions were common among the palace women in the capital). Today, he said, things have changed. He suggested three reasons: the Japanese efforts to break the custom, the greater freedom of contact between men and women, and the fact that boys no longer wear their hair long like girls. Yet still the colloquial description of a good-looking boy is 'pretty, like a girl' and implies no disparagement.

The last generation has seen some changes in the formal relations between the sexes, but the men still walk ahead of the women; men chat in one room and women in another; and men go out to enjoy themselves while women stay at home. Sexuality is more of a necessity than a pleasure.

I always enjoy my visits to the chapel at Tŏguri. The food is so good there. Food differs from village to village. At Gull's Ferry it is always poor, sometimes only boiled shrimps and barley. At Tŏguri it is good, even though the materials are neither rare nor costly. This is because there used to be an aristocratic house in the village, and the people learned new ideas from the kitchen of the *yangban,* or aristocrat. The great house has gone now. Only part of it remains, and that part in ruins.

I have been talking about it to the catechist. He was married when he was fourteen, only thirty years ago. That was when he put up his topknot. Then he came to live here a little later and run the village school, an old-style one for learning

Chinese. So many things have changed since then. In those days Tŏguri was an important place on a main road. That's how the English fathers from Suwŏn came to build a church there. Then the Japanese built their new roads and railways away from the old centres, so that Japanese people could acquire property on the new communication routes. The old aristocrats mostly melted away. He remarked that you never see a donkey nowadays. In the old days aristocrats used to ride donkeys. So did merchants.

But back to the food. This is the kind of village where they understand all twelve flavours in an ox's head and how to cook the leaves of the wild sesame. This time we had a delicious cold soup of eggplant, peppers, and mussels. Sometimes it is octopus and ginger. Often it is seaweed, sometimes with tiny potatoes. I think it is in soups that Korean cooking really excels; and it is the skill of the cook in making the blend that counts, because these soups have no names and are not made according to formal recipes.

Korean food is not bland like the Japanese. It is strong-flavoured. Nor does it concern itself with appearance for appearance's sake. There are no added colourings like the pink in Japanese ginger and the pale green in Japanese whipped egg-white. A Korean meal-table is colourful because eggs are yellow, peppers are scarlet, and greens are green. All these things are served primarily for their taste. There are no inedible garnishes. Moreover, the meal sits comfortably on the stomach, and there is no reason (in spite of the American doctors) why you should not eat any or all of it. I eat excellent water snails on occasion and sometimes even fresh-water crabs. Most village well-water is all right. The bacteriologists have tried several times, but they have found no parasites in me yet.

There's been a good deal of rain lately. They say it always rains on the seventh night of the seventh moon, which was thought to be my birthday by the lunar calendar, so I had to eat seaweed soup for breakfast. It's an old Oriental festival, celebrating the star Vega under the name of the Spinning Maiden. She is deeply in love with a star called the Herd Boy, but their romance hinders their work, so they are separated by the Milky Way, and allowed to meet just once a year on this night. The magpies fly up to make a bridge for them to cross the river of the Milky Way, and tonight's rain is their tears as they have to part.

The maize is high above my head in the dry fields. The rice is all standing green; soon it will be in flower. The gourd flowers are white on the roofs, and the floppy orange flowers of the squash sprawl over all the banks and waste places. King-fishers and dragonflies, in two shades of metallic blue, dart over the ditches and brooks, enhancing the deeper, purer blue of the flowers of the Korean chickweed sprawling on every bank. The tall pink lilies that Americans call 'naked ladies' looked beautiful with hibiscus on the plain little altar at Tŏguri when I said this month's mass there. The leaves of the lily plants disappear before the flowers bloom, and old T'aekhwa gave me a Chinese verse saying 'Leaves and flowers never meet . . .'

Jacob is out of the army at last, and it was good to have him serving the altar. He is young and good-looking, the adopted son of the dour widow Susanna who really rules my flock in Tŏguri. She generally has some grumbles, if not downright scolding, for me too, and there's the devil to pay if I don't eat enough of the rice she cooks for me. Jacob is married and has a toddler son. Another baby is expected soon. Jacob has been away about two years in the army, and while he was away Susanna and her daughter-in-law somehow or other tilled their fields and fed their pigs and kept the family going. They had some help from outside, and I dare say that Susanna dragooned it efficiently. As I came home today I met the gaunt

Susanna and the erect Jacob on the field path. His neatly pressed uniform is gone for good, and he was barefooted for work, but his fineboned face still shows the lines of good stock. Poor farmers are by no means poor-spirited in Korea.

A priest who visited me last week had seen two fatal bus accidents on the road. Slightly shaken, he remarked that this seems to be the season for them.

Like most Koreans, but (I gather) few foreigners, I have to rely on buses for travelling. Almost no one in our half of the county owns a jeep, and I know of not a single car. We must use the buses that go eight or nine times a day along the road westward from the county town through our village, and on for another five miles to a derelict fishing and ferry port by the sea. They are the total service for our heavily populated 'Four Myŏn (Rural Districts) Beyond the Water', and they are never less than crowded.

Until this spring two very small buses ran a shuttle service. Passengers travelled like condemned prisoners in a concentration camp: in winter bitterly cold, in summer dusty and stifled, stuffed in so tightly that you could scarcely move an arm. The one nightmare that village life held for me was that ghastly ten miles in the lurching bus. There was no need to dwell on the dangers. Stumbling over the bumpy road, we risked death in many forms: had the bus turned over in the flooded paddies we must have drowned; had a fire started, few could have escaped. It is a little better now. There are several buses, and the new ones are bigger, but they are still too full for safety.

At the county town bus station there is a constant coming and going of buses up and down the main road. Most of them roar and splutter to a stop with a groan which suggests they will never start again. There is a lively competition by conductresses for passengers and by passengers for seats.

When our village bus comes in, there is a rush for both

doors. The youthful conductors fight off the passengers in an effort to empty the bus before attempting to refill it. There is always a free fight. The women are always more frantic than the men, yet only grandfathers ever actually climb in through the windows. Self-defence, as well as self-interest, has led me to adopt my own technique, which differs from the others' chiefly in that I do not waste energy in shouting. There seems to be no restriction as to the amount of luggage a person can bring aboard. Women bring huge aluminium bowls of laundry, bags of grain, live chickens, sometimes even a small pig. Once I was travelling in a bus when there was great to-do over the paraphernalia of a sorceress clambering aboard with her drums and gongs and trident.

I have little real need to worry about getting a place. Even if I am eventually projected into the bus after every seat is taken, it is a rare day when no one gives up his seat to the foreign guest. Generally it is a schoolboy, a policeman, or a soldier. Nor is it a matter of respect for my cloth, because it happens as often when the heat compels me to wear an open-necked shirt and the shoeshine boys call me 'Uncle', as it does when I travel in a black suit and Roman collar. However, 'Uncle' or 'Father', once seated, you must travel like the rest: wet fish indecently clad in scanty straw wisps under your knees, a bag of grain at your feet, a schoolboy between your shoulder blades, live chickens on your lap, and an elbow in your face. A bundle of dubious contents in a Japanese kerchief, including a badly corked bottle, may descend on any part of you at any time. Once I was showered with a confetti of tiny pink shrimps. But why, oh why, will someone—who invariably sits just behind me—always choose the most crowded day to pose knotty problems about denominational differences, in Korean and in public?

Fellow travellers and bus crews are rarely reserved. Often their conversation is interesting. Thus I heard from one grimy little driver's mate how he worked on a 150-mile run, sleeping in the bus company's dormitories and never seeing his family oftener than once a month; and from a boy conductor of the temptations involved in handling daily far more money than he earned in a month. And there are the passengers. Scarcely do I board a bus without seeing someone refuse to pay the proper fare, taking advantage of the conductor's youth. The sums involved are generally so small that were I not a foreigner it would give me great pleasure to pay them.

Two notices say 'No Smoking' and 'Don't chat with the driver.' Although written in Korean script, and therefore readable by all, they are habitually ignored. So are many other safety precautions. Last month I was in a bus which had a race with another on a curving main road. The danger was horrifying. The driver clenched his teeth, and the conductress feverishly hustled passengers at stops, while some of the passengers spurred the game on. The terror ceased only when we were so long delayed at a halt that the other machine gained an indisputable lead.

At least I must give our local enterprises credit for not using buses such as I have seen in other places, where the springs of the accelerator and foot brake are replaced by elastic rubber strips attached to the steering column, and the radiator's thirst has constantly to be slaked with water from the rice fields.

The main roads are more or less regularly made up. In some provinces subsidiary roads are also kept in good order, but not in our district. Our roads were once dressed with rock, which theoretically needs no attention. So we have a hundred yards of rock-hopping and a hundred yards of mud-wallowing. The bridges are made to match. Every one of them begins and ends with a six-inch step, and most have gaps or rotting timbers. I expect they will be mended after something falls through.

The journey is always entertaining, from the helpful passengers, through the scruffy vendors who come aboard at towns, to the constant fascination of the countryside. Nevertheless, I shall continue to commit my journeys most devoutly to my guardian angel.

Last week the village postmaster's father died. Quite apart from the dignity of his son's office, he had been a noted local scholar, living several miles away in a pretty hamlet called Chestnut Vale. I had not been able to go to the funeral (which had in any case been a pagan one) but a visit of condolence was called for a couple of days later.

I went with an old Christian scholar. The afternoon sunshine was bright and warm. The standing rice, still green but with the seedheads swelling, gave off a pleasant fragrance in the heat. The pine trees also gave a heavy scent, and the chestnut-leaved oaks were full of crickets and cicadas whose shrill grating and screeching deafened us whenever we passed through the shade of a grove. The tall seedheads of the sorghum waved gently in the breeze. In the hamlets the fruit was beginning to form on the jujube and persimmon trees. The peppers were reddening in the gardens, and the flowers of the domesticated sesame were dropping so that the seed pods could swell. The field sesame had no flowers yet, but if you crushed its leaves in the fingers you had another of the characteristic good scents of the Korean summer. On the thatched roofs of the houses the swelling gourds loomed like pale green moons among their dark leaves studded with the white stars of the flowers. Hardly anyone was to be seen in the peaceful countryside. Everything shimmered slightly, in sabbatical quiet under a bright blue sky.

The house of the dead man was typical, built of red clay and heavily thatched. In the yard in front of it, straw and cut grass were spread out to dry in the sun. (The countryside is spattered now with notices in Chinese telling us to increase our production of this economical kind of fuel.) A group of pullets, dominated by a finely barred grey-and-fawn cock with brilliant wattles, was scratching about there.

The dead man's sons, dressed in the elaborate sackcloth clothes that custom requires, met us at the door of the reception room, the only door of the house which gives directly on to the outside roads. They knelt on rough straw bundles set on a very coarse straw mat on the verandah beside the door. We went into the room to pay our respects while they cried out with the ceremonial wails.

There was a table set before the spirit chair, canopied and curtained with white linen. In the chair was a photograph of the dead man, wearing his indoor hat. His face had a kindly expression which I have some to associate with these country scholars. On the walls were twenty or so white silk banners, covered with Chinese inscriptions in his honour. Some were in verse, and some in excellent calligraphy. Several of them made play on the fact that he had died in the seventh moon of his seventy-seventh year. The simple, less elegantly written banner from the middle school stood out in stark contrast to the old-world perfection of the others. Among them hung his outdoor hat. In the chair, beside the photograph, was a white paper envelope with the Chinese character for 'top' (*sang*) written on it, standing on its end. This substitute for the spirit tablet containing the man's name contained instead, I was told, the folded collar strip from one of his Korean-style coats.

On the table was a sacrifice of fruit, rice cakes, and dried fish on dishes with stems, together with a pale-grey glazed porcelain incense burner. There were two brass candlesticks and two piles of envelopes, one of telegrams and one of money gifts. There were also the dead man's pipe and fan. We put down our small gift of money, wrapped in an envelope on which we had written in Chinese 'To comfort sorrow', and stepped back onto the verandah.

The sons came forward and sat on a finely woven grass mat to drink a cup of cloudy rice beer, served with a few titbits among which pieces of American canned beef seemed very out of place. There was smoking. (The postmaster's lighter has a Chinese inscription on it.) To ease the heat we were offered the fan from the sacrifice table in the room. It was a big folding one of glazed black paper. A line of gilt calligraphy on it read: 'Spring rains wash a fair face,' but no one could decide exactly what that signified. I was told that the fan had not been burned along with the rest of the father's personal belongings because it is not now easy to buy anything of such good quality.

Over the door, on paper yellow with age, were two fine heavy characters meaning peace and harmony. Between them was a little square of new white paper with the character for 'big river' written on it, but upside down. There was a little embarrassment on the part of my companion while the postmaster, without embarrassment, explained that all that water coming down was a protection against fire.

We talked for half an hour, until the next guest arrived. As he went inside and bowed his forehead to the floor before the photograph, we left for home. The sons continued with their wailing and their entertaining. They will maintain the sacrifice in front of the spirit chair for three years.

SEPTEMBER

秋
涼

MIDDAY is still summery, and we wear light clothes, but the nights and mornings are already autumnal. The warm floor chills before people wake, and the sun remains a white disc in the mist until it gets high in the sky. Already I have heard the cliché quoted that now is the season of 'high sky and plump horses', though we have not a single horse in the village or anywhere near by. We consider them urban creatures. The booths are being taken down in the cucumber fields. The rice fields have been drained, and their emerald colour is tarnished with a dull silvery sheen, a prelude to the gold of the harvest. Here and there is a brownish patch where the fine glutinous rice used for the best cakes and wine is growing.

The village is gay with mats of scarlet peppers drying in the sun by the roadside or spread out on the thatched roofs. Other roofs have a temporary double thatch where the broom grass that will give us next year's stock of besoms is drying. And everywhere pyramids of sesame stems stand like stacked rifles, gradually turning from olive green to black. The morning-glory is rivalled by the rich mauve of the Michaelmas daisies in the cottage gardens. We are entering into the season the Koreans love best.

Sunday was the Autumn Moon Festival. It has a Korean name, Han-gawi, as well as the Chinese name Ch'usŏk, meaning Autumn Evening. I asked a country scholar why it should

113

be called evening. He did not exactly answer my question, but he gave me a quotation declaring that the mid-autumn nights are so lovely that they bring to mind the golden age of Yao and Shun, for which Confucius himself waxed nostalgic. Certainly the village lost all its cares for the weekend. If you ever doubted what a *fête champêtre* could be, you should come to the country for Ch'usŏk.

It all started on the previous market day, when there was a bumper crowd and booming trade. More cows, more apples, more seaweed, more fish, more quacks, more people. It was a festival in itself. I met a harassed young teacher, using a schoolboy as intermediary, trying to bargain for a chicken. The village bank was crowded; you could scarcely get into the post office for the rush. The word *myŏngjŏl* (festival) was on everyone's lips.

Then came the preparations in the kitchen, especially of the little half-moon-shaped rice cakes, stuffed with beans and flavoured with pine needles, which are the appropriate thing for the time. And there was travelling. Student sons and daughters came home; some families sent representatives away to visit 'the big house' (the senior house of that branch of the family). One young man told me that really only the children can enjoy Ch'usŏk, but he had patently caught the excitement himself.

Meanwhile the moon, the cause of it all, was nearing her perfection. Michael and I went to the top of the old beacon hill to get the best view. As she rode clear in a flawless sky, dusting the undulating hills with platinum, and reflected in the ruffled pool at our feet, it was easy to dream of Yao and Shun. From every valley around, voices rose clear in the night air. One young man was singing his heart out in a sentimental Irish song. In another direction a group were crooning Korean songs. From hamlet after hamlet came the insistent throbbing rhythm of the farmers' bands: gongs, pipes, and cymbals. Some children's voices were raised in a festival game. Politics and war seemed so unreal that even the winking lights of the distant aerodrome became just a part of the beauty of the scene.

Come the morning of the feast, the shops are all shut. It is one of those rare days when the village wears a Sunday-morning air. Everyone dons his best, whether it be a carefully ironed Korean coat or a dapper Western suit. Even the men who usually wear grubby Western trousers turn out in Korean clothes with gay ankle-ribbons and waistcoats of flowered silk. The women wear their national dress almost without exception.

The day's first duty is to the dead. The burial places have all been cleared of the summer's growth of weeds, and non-Christians go to sacrifice at the newer graves. It is our custom in this village to have requiem masses in the church. After breakfast we walked up the hillside to the fresh green mound which is the grave of the last parish priest and there prayed for his soul and sang an Easter hymn. I am glad that our Christians have not despised and thrown off their piety for the departed.

I had so many invitations to eat out—mostly given on the morning itself—that I had to select and make the fairest rounds I could. In one family the third son was celebrating his first hundred days, so he had to be visited. Among the pine cakes at his party were big chunks of snow-white rice bread, the correct thing for that occasion. Then I was to bless a new well in another village, in the house of a scholar. Again there were piles of pine cakes and, as a special curiosity, spicy Chinese moon-cakes, wrapped in crimson paper, sent in as a gift from the Chinese house in the village. (Like most Korean villages, ours has a chop-house run by a family of Shantung Chinese.)

The scholars were showing discreet enthusiasm for President Rhee's recently announced Chinese poetry contest. And in the midst of the feast the lads of the village appeared outside the door with drums and gongs, making a noise such as the 150th Psalm suggests. They were wearing their best clothes but nothing extraordinary. A handsome lad in blue trousers and a white shirt with overlong sleeves was dancing. The movements of his wrists were very graceful, but the rest of the choreography was chiefly abandon and heel stepping. There are still people who can dance spontaneously when they are happy.

Back home in the evening our rustic Gregorian chant at Benediction was accompanied from outside by yet more of this strangely thrilling music. It went on until long after the moon was up again.

Next day was the school sports. Thousands came from miles around to show off their best clothes under the bunting and enjoy the blare of the loudspeaker system's music and occasionally to watch the races. Ice-cake vendors came from far away with large boxes strapped on their bicycles. The schoolyard was fringed under all the trees with men sitting on the ground selling peaches and apples and bottled drinks. There was dust and colour and noise and gaiety. In front of the school was the marquee with distinguished guests and a tableful of prizes: notebooks for the children and useful pots and pans and towels for the grownups. As is inevitable in this mystic and non-materialistic Orient, the top front edge of the tent was fringed with paper saying how much money each subscriber to the event had given.

There were races for everybody, mostly run on bare feet. The major battle was between the white and blue teams of the school. (In Japanese days they were red and blue. Red has now been dropped for political reasons.) There were also more entertaining things than mere running. The local ladies had an exciting needle-threading race, the distinguished guests dribbled a mammoth football, and the girls had a race between teams preparing tables of food. There was plenty of hilarity.

It lasted all day, and came to its climax just before dusk when a hundred girls appeared on the ground to perform a Korean palace dance (or at least, so they call it here). It was simple, and the more sophisticated onlookers criticized it severely. Nevertheless the mass of crimson, scarlet and purple skirts set off by the brilliant yellow bodices, all enlivened by the fluttering of the long white overhand sleeves, was a charming sight. It also increased my respect for the country schoolteachers who produced it.

But the colour and excitement of autumn are not over yet. Next market day we begin a great contest of the morris dances and farmers' bands, together with wrestling bouts. The prizes are bulls, but the publicity is very vague. Some people think it will last for five days. I hope it does. Meanwhile the school children are having a short holiday to get over the exertions of their sports day.

Next Friday is Confucius's birthday. I dare say that very few of the people hereabouts will remember the fact. Yet no influence lies stronger on our countryside than that of the Confucian schoolmen of Sung times, who provided the guiding ideals of the Yi dynasty.

It is dangerous, especially for the unlearned, to point to any particular activity or way of thought and say, 'That is Confucian,' because the legacy of Confucius is so intimately welded with much that had its origin both before and after the sage's own teaching. It is equally difficult not to be trite in saying anything about Confucianism. I have an English-speaking Korean friend who habitually refers to 'Confucianism, which foreigners say is not a religion. . . . ' But I find that the phrase which would sum up the attitude of the self-confessed Confucian literati of my acquaintance in the parish is 'The sage did not speak of wonders, great feats, or spirits.' They have gently cynical calm and an unequalled poise of mind.

It would also probably be fair to attribute to the lingering influence of Confucius the fantastic eagerness which everybody has for education. Everyone who knows Korea even a little knows the sacrifices which people are prepared to make to educate the sons of the family, often to achieve a result that is out of all proportion disappointing. And can it be the same respect for learning for its own sake that makes paper and writing materials (usually notebooks and pencils) the most acceptable gift or prize for the village boys?

Then if Confucianism means veneration for the family line and especially for father, Confucianism is very much with us. Even the moderately Westernized shopkeeper or official in my village still has this feeling in his very blood. You see it in the extreme reluctance with which a young man will accept a cup of wine in the presence of his father, then finally turn his face into the corner and gulp it down with embarrassment. You see it in the regular performance of the deep bow, with forehead to the floor, which is still common among young men. (Like other foreigners of my acquaintance, I found this greeting at first highly embarrassing, until I realized that there is not much else you can do before a man who is himself already sitting on the floor. And there was the youth who hesitated a long time while I sat expectantly. Finally he said, 'Please sit straight so I can bow to you.')

You can see the same spirit in the local monuments. There are at least three kinds of these, and they all tend to be outside or on the edge of the village. First there is the memorial stone, a simple pillar with an inscription recording someone's filial piety, or expressing the gratitude of the people who benefited from a dead man's bounty, or praising a widow who remained faithful to her husband's memory. Often it is sheltered by a little pavilion with a tiled roof, the pillars painted red, and all enclosed with fine wooden bars. Then there is the red gate memorial. This is nobler than a mere stone because it could be erected only when granted by royal decree. The inscription is painted on a red board like the lintel of a gate, and it is kept in a small pavilion like a memorial stone, or even in a full-sized spirit-shrine along with sacrificial paraphernalia.

There are two or three real shrines in my parish. They are at least as big as a house, and stand in a small walled terrain with a triple gate in front. The best of them is that of Sin Suk-chu, the famous fifteenth-century prime minister and diplomat whose skill in foreign languages is proverbial. He was one of the scholars who worked on the preparation of the Korean alphabet, but he has lost the favour of posterity because he later supported the usurping uncle who murdered the tragic boy king, Tanjong. His name has become a colloquial word for the hard green beans which are now drying in baskets in front of many of the cottages; their shoots grow twisted like his heart. His shrine is small and simple but relatively well kept by his descendants, who populate the little village. It contains a fine large silk-scroll painting of him dressed in emerald-green robes. The family will willingly show it to any visitor, but after unrolling it, and before doing it up again, they reverence it with their deepest bows. They will not take it outside to be photographed. They keep up regular sacrifices. The place is in no sense spooky, but he would be a dull soul who could feel no sense of reverence there.

The pattern of the building is repeated, on a larger scale and with more splendid buildings, at the two local *hyanggyo*, the old shrines of Confucius himself. In front there is the Hall for Illuminating the Relationships (Myŏngnyun-dang), which was the discussion and study room and also served as a vestry for ceremonies. Then a flight of stone steps leads to the triple gates of the walled enclosure in which stands the Hall of Great Perfection (Taesŏng-jŏn). Within the latter are the tablets of Confucius, Mencius, and the other canonized sages recognized in Korea. Here in spring and autumn, on days marked Snake in the calendar, sacrifice used to be offered. Here were the spiritual centres of the two old counties of Chinwi and P'yŏng-t'aek which have gone to make our one modern P'yŏngt'aek county.

119

A short time ago I went to visit the shrine at Chinwi. Older people who do not live on the spot still call it 'the old town', but now there is only a small village, called Pongnam, well off any main road, on the north side of a beautiful rice valley. The temple is a little beyond the village, halfway up the hillside in a grove of chestnut-leaved oaks, at the head of a tiny valley facing south. The place has been very carefully selected so as to gain good 'Wind and Water' influences, according to Chinese geomantic principles.

The Hall for Illuminating the Relationships is in a poor way and needs repair. (This has been the state of several such temples that I have visited. The old P'yŏngt'aek one, at Kaeksari, has become a dwelling.) The place used to be kept up on the revenue of its ricelands, but modern land reform removed that source of income. It seems that Confucius has suffered more than Buddha in this respect.

Inside the main hall all is at least clean and tidy, though new paint and new paper for the windows are sadly needed. The tablets stand around in their chairs, each covered with a wooden box-like preserver. The central one bears the inscription 'Great Perfect All-Holy Prince of Illustrious Learning' (if indeed it is genuinely translatable at all). The sacrificial vessels, of which there are many (round bowls, flat dishes, and three-legged wine cups), are all made of brass with self-consciously unpolished workmanship. The brass is poor. They used to be better before the Japanese took them for melting down during the world war.

There are a number of books, some in manuscript. They are mostly rites and registers. The preface of one, printed during the Japanese period, mentions that even Westerners had felt compelled to recognize the nobility of Confucius' teachings. The whole place smells musty, but saddest of all is the sight of the rector's blue robes and black cap, eaten by moths and mildew. The big purple tassel will soon be parted from the great horn belt, and before long the hat will be unusable.

The local gentry will be out on Friday, I was told, when the sacrifice is made—no longer a spring and autumn affair, but an annual birthday celebration for the sage, on the twenty-seventh day of the eighth moon. The rector will preside and a few seniors will gather, dressed in their pleated coats (*top'o*) to take up their places east and west in the tiny courtyard, to honour the greatest of sages. I am sorry I shall not be able to go and watch them.

The boys of the village thought the temple a dull place to visit. They insisted on a visit to the garish bodhisattvas of a little Buddhist monastery that of 'the Myriad Miracles', a couple of miles further up the valley. The Buddhist shrine is a jolly home for a monk and his family. Its history is long, but its atmosphere is nil.

I preferred Confucius, even in his decay. I see a great appropriateness in the fact that the Christian word for saint is exactly the same as the Confucian word for sage. And I was much moved by my old Christian friend who walked into the temple, made the sign of the cross, and prayed. He said afterwards, 'I was thanking God for the light he gave to the people of the East before they learned about Christ.'

Publicity for our dance and wrestling festival got under way in the end. Handwritten posters appeared, announcing exact lists of prizes: useful things like bulls, spades, bolts of cloth, and towels. It was sponsored by our Market Development Committee, again functioning as the traditional Korean village guild for the 'comfort of the aged'.

Only three teams of dancers out of a possible forty or so in the area turned up. Some of the others could not afford the necessary finery, but some were regrettably cowardly. Those that did come arrived dancing behind their banners. They visited the shrine of the tutelary spirit of the village and danced there. They danced through the village, and they danced till it grew dark in the market place.

Then flares were lit, and the wrestling contest got under way. It was the traditional Korean kind. Two men strip to the waist and stand barefooted in an arena of deep sand. They lock, bent over, each with one hand round his opponent's back and the other round his thigh. They may grip one another's trousers, or they may tie a band of hempen cloth around the waist and thigh to give a hold. They struggle and strain until one of them is thrown off balance and falls. The bouts are very short. The two smallest boys begin. The winner takes on the next in size, and so on. The youngsters, if they threw three opponents, got prizes: pencils and notebooks. The elders were eliminated in a series of heats for bigger prizes of clothing and tools, and finally the bull.

I think everybody really enjoyed the music and dancing more. After two extended performances on the second day, we knew all about the three competing teams when it came to the judgement on the third evening. First there was the group from the village called Pangnim, 'Fragrant Forest'. Their average age was young. They had eight dancers and two hourglass-shaped drums as well as the usual collection of gongs and pipes. Their turnout was a bit ragged, but they were pleasant and likeable. Then there was the Bridgeport team. They were the biggest of all and had the oldest men. Their leader has a Presidential prize, won in a national contest. Their trappings were pink and yellow, and the foaming silk ruching on their foreheads was all in a vivid deep pink: the shade cardinals are supposed to wear on Rose Sunday. The third team was from Forge Valley. They were a 4-H Club, so they were the youngest of all. Their bandoliers were all red; their headdresses carried big white flowers stuck in the scarlet silk. Their leader was a modest little man with a charming smile.

After a parade round the village, Fragrant Forest led off.

Their energy was prodigious. They kicked up as much dust as a rodeo. Their swivelled hat tassels were aiming at *perpetuum mobile*. The audience broke out into ecstatic clapping whenever the boys were standing in a circle swirling their tassels in figures of eight while the percussion beat *sforzando accelerando.* For nearly an hour they danced—in circles, in lines, in figures; on the spot, in procession, or squatting on the ground. Always their high point was the youngest of all, a boy with a baby-fresh face wearing twice as many bandoliers as anyone else and leaping twice as high.

There were two breaks in the performance: one while the drummers did their own display, dancing and drumming with faces of ecstatic smiling joy; then the pipes produced a special tune, and two of the boys put on swivelled hats made of straw without brims, whose chin straps they held in their teeth but whose tassels were streamers fifty feet long. With a flick of the hand they had them swirling, up and around, over their heads and under their feet, or horizontally like lariats. They knelt, they crawled, they danced, they sat, but always the great paper streamer was kept in movement. This was exciting.

At last they were finished, and without a break in the music Forge Valley appeared in the arena behind their banner, which carried the 4-H flag as well, and was borne by a man in a conical hat with a grotesque face painted on the front and 'March North and Unite' on the back. They were the smallest troupe. They too had a dimpled Benjamin at their tail. They also had a one-eyed lad who put up a most creditable performance. They tried no fancy tricks, but they danced their full hour. Their leader was the most magnificent of all and might have been taken for a Mongol general. (Now I am not sure exactly what a Mongol general would in fact have looked like, but in watching this performance I could not help thinking that part of the history of this dancing must be military. The brassbound hat is military; some of the terms used are military; the marching movements and the horselike prancing of the

123

leaders smack more of the camp than of the farm. I wonder whether in fact there is any connection with Mongol levies. People who have visited Mongolia say they have seen similar dances at Ulaan Bator.)

Forge Valley were best in the adagio movements; because, though they did not lack vigour, their prestissimo (of which there was plenty) lacked co-ordination. When their time was up, there was a sense of disappointment. They hadn't the polish of Fragrant Forest, but they had pluck and were good sports, and we had enjoyed their performance. It was unpleasant to know they could not possibly win.

Then Bridgeport came out. It was getting dark. I still cannot make up my mind whether they were playing fair or not. In the dusk it was hard to see their timing, but by now the din and rhythm were intoxicating. The reputation of their leader counted for much. He carried things further by a virtuoso display with an even larger swivelled-hat streamer which he put on with nice showmanship. He outdid Fragrant Forest's drummers in a dance with two other drummers in which he played all three drums at once, in which he drummed while rotating and running at high speed with a technique in *fouetté* which a ballerina might envy and in percussion which might turn green the doped virtuosi of New York's night clubs.

Then by the light of the flares his troupe took to spectacle. He mounted on another man's shoulders and sang a farmers' song, swaying as they all danced holding ribbons attached to his waist. They burst paper globes to release many coloured ribbons along with streamers praising Korea and the U.N. Finally they did a long ballet of the whole process of rice culture from the seeding to the threshing and the storing of the grain. It was splendid, and let no townsman dare to call it primitive. There was a final ear-splitting parade, before the swirling ribbons left the arena, and we were reduced to watching the altogether gentler sport of wrestling until the results could be announced.

There really were no results to announce. It was all so obvious. Yet no one had the heart to send Forge Valley 4-H Club back home with the third prize of a bolt of cloth. Most people would dearly have loved to give them the two bulls of the first prize. Their pluck deserved it if not their technique. So the village elders sat up till long after midnight, and at last arrived at a just conclusion. Bridgeport were obviously semi-professional and dazzled us with specialities. So they had to be labelled 'Special Class' and get a special prize. Fragrant Forest deserved first prize and got the two bulls; but Forge Valley 4-H Club had second prize, so they will get a bull too—which was what we all wanted.

OCTOBER

菊
秋

THE AUTUMN building season is on us. After dark the air is filled with the rhythmic chant of men preparing a site for a house, and now buildings are springing up all around our new market place. Before long our market village will be claiming town status. Several of the new buildings are two-storeyed These upper storeys, ill-constructed and with badly-made stairs, are strictly for prestige purposes, and afford no practical advantage. A new protestant chapel is also going up, in the inevitable grim grey cement with the inevitable useless steeple. It replaces a little thatched hall which was certainly easier to keep warm. Was ever a fair countryside so disfigured by these ugly conventicles as are the Korean hills? But the tower has prestige value. One might think that the village was prospering. I suspect that it is.

On the last market day I walked out to one of my more distant chapelries, at Gull Ferry, a village which even an ox-cart cannot reach. The roads and paths were thronged with people coming and going, the brilliant sunshine dazzlingly reflected on their clean white clothes. It occurred to me for the first time during that two hours' solitary walk that in spite of the whole complex reticulation of this countryside by paths and roads across the fields and through the woods, I never passed through a single hamlet. The path always skirted the settlements. This is generally true of the whole area. To go from one village to another you do not pass through a third, unless you use a motor road.

The rice is mostly formed now, and some of it is being harvested with sickles, but the colour of the fields in the smaller valleys is still only a yellowish green, and even the broader stretches are barely golden yet. Although there is a certain amount of the disease that shrivels and burns the seed heads, the farmers are generally satisfied with their rice crop.

Fruit, on the other hand, has done badly. We have less good fruit in the village than there is in the towns. The chestnuts are very poor, and some of the persimmons have not done at all well. In one village I was given a welcome with persimmons, both partially ripened ones which had been marinaded for a day in brine, and the soft luscious fully ripened ones called 'soft persimmons' (*yŏnsi*). Finally I was sent off with a branch of leaves and fruit to hang in my study while the fruit ripens. The persimmon tree is said to have seven excellences: long life, much shade, no birds' nests, no grubs and insects, beauty after the frost, fair fruit, and leaves which can be used for writing on. Now is its peak season.

The gourds are about to be cut; the squash has mostly been cut already, and slices of it lie drying in the sun with the various kinds of beans, sesame, and the crimson peppers that brighten the thatched roofs of the cottages. There are giant russet marigolds and flaming zinnias still in the cottage yards, and the pink and white of the straggly cosmos brightens the verges of the main roads.

The farmhouses are deserted at midday because everybody is out at work. I ate my lunch in the shade of the verandah while a piglet grunted contentedly in one corner of the yard and a few hens pattered about among the shrimps and peppers laid out in the sunshine. Above me a handful of vivid cape-gooseberries were hanging from the beam, waiting to be used for medicine. The old wall clock ticked comfortably in the inner room.

By evening the village began to be noisier and livelier. The sun set in a blaze of gilt-edged clouds. The children came home, and the little ones ran in with offerings of freshly filched persimmons and barely ripe chestnuts. The smell of wood smoke permeated the village for a short time while the evening meal was being cooked.

I found a pleasant youth sitting with a sickle grasped firmly between the soles of his bare feet. He was taking handfuls of grass and turnip tops and cutting them into small pieces. It was the cow's supper, being prepared to be boiled. 'These cold nights,' he said, 'she needs hot food.' The Japanese, it was explained, tired to stop the practice of boiling animals' fodder, but the animals suffered and grew thin, so the custom has been resumed . . .

A fat white puppy was irritating its mother. The hens were carrying out a bootless inspection of the thatch among the gourd vines. The birds had congregated in the poplars and were making a noise like a parrot house. This is a Korea which reeks of history; but lest we should get too starry-eyed over it, during breakfast next morning I was accompanied by the ballet music of Tchaikovski's *Sleeping Princess* on the wireless.

I have been musing on our local history and particularly on the names of these villages. In spite of assiduous searching, I have so far failed to trace any study of the history of Korean place names, or any recognition in an English-language book of the fact that many villages have several names, some Korean and some Sino-Korean.

It would seem reasonable to suppose that the Korean names are older. They generally have some simple geographical meaning: Springwater Valley, Big Hollow, Chestnut Village, and so forth. Others are named after fancied resemblance of geographic features to various objects: Tiger Rock, Dragon's

Head, Forge Valley, Hat Hill, and such like. All these have corresponding versions translated into Chinese characters for normal written purposes, but the Korean name (it is often in a dialect or archaic form) is mostly used in conversation. Some of the bigger villages have Sino-Korean names only. Their meanings tend to be moral or poetic: Centre of Peace, Mutual Trust, Sans Souci.

A few Sino-Korean names are not translations of the Korean but transliterations. Thus our *tume*, meaning a mountain hamlet, is written with two Chinese characters of similar sound but meaning Great Bear Constellation and plum blossom (a meaning in itself auspicious). Saptari is half transliterated and half translated into two Chinese characters pronounced Sapkyo. The first character means to thread, but sounds like *sap*, while the second one translates the Korean *tari* and means a bridge.

Forgotten meanings and mistakes occur. Thus Nŭji has been rendered by Chinese characters meaning late (suggested by the sound of *nŭ*), and lake (suggested by the sound of *ji*) and called Manho; and Soenuri, 'the place where the cows lie down', used to be called in Sino-Korean Wauri, which has the same meaning, but has had its name changed by a complex pun on the words for cow and gold into the better-sounding Kŭmgongni: Golden Vale. This is said, most unreliably, to have been done about a century ago. There is some fascinating work to be done in the unravelling of rural place names.

Modern national holidays are sometimes observed in the village with a parade of officials and a brief ceremony with speeches. More often they go unobserved. So it was not surprising that I forgot the holiday and arrived in Seoul on National Foundation Day, when I could do little of the business I had planned. What better, then, than go to the Confucian university and see the revived Paegilchang, the national poetry contest? It was an appropriate excursion for one up from the country, since most of the participants were from the provinces, and the old style literati of my village had been discussing it ever since the first announcement in the newspapers, which I heard about at Ch'usŏk, a month ago.

The courtyard behind the tablet house of the Sŏnggyun-gwan, where the big ginkgo trees are, was filled with a gay crowd of men and women. There were many students of the Confucian university; there was a fair sprinkling of country scholars; there were large numbers of women. The sunshine was glorious. Two enclaves had been made in the court. On the right, under the zelkova tree, was the place where the competitors in the classical Chinese style were sitting, with their ink bottles and large sheaves of paper, on straw mats set on the ground. Most wore the common white Korean coat, but one had a pale blue pleated coat (top'o), and a few had scholars' caps (yugŏn). The average age must have been well over sixty, though one man might have been in his forties. The faces of these old men were nearly all marked with the kind gentility that their kind of education instils. Fifty had been selected from the four thousand entries which had come in from all over the country for the preliminary contest. A few of the fifty had failed to turn up.

On the left hand side, under the pine trees, were the offerers of *sijo*, the classical Korean-language verse form. The average age was much lower. There were even a few schoolboys. Again, if faces are a reliable guide, one would be tempted to think that the practice of poetry has a good effect upon the character. There had been rather more than one thousand entries for this half of the contest. To judge by the ages of the competitors and the relative number of entrants, it looks as though the art of composing Chinese verses must soon die in Korea, while the national form of disciplined verse is unlikely to achieve the vogue which Chinese composition had in the past.

After brief introductory speeches (and much fussing) the subject for the day's competition was announced, written on

131

a board, and displayed at the top of the steps in front of the Myŏngnyun-dang. The President had proposed for the title of the poem 'Thoughts on Reading of the Japanese Invasion of 1592', a subject at once traditional and topical. For the executants of Chinese verse, however, there was an additional complication. His Excellency also provided the rhymes. According to the custom of these contests, the poets must incorporate these rhyming characters into their poems in certain rigidly prescribed places. This time the rhyme characters meant: among, loyal, empty, palace, hero.

They fell to composing, inspiration coming more quickly to some than to others. I was rather shocked to see some of the old gentlemen consulting dictionaries of characters and lists of rhymes—a thing my village friends would consider disgraceful. They had two hours for the job. When the poems were finished they were brush-written and thrown over a white screen at the top of the steps. My companion and I circulated a little, saluting some friends, before we retired for lunch. It seemed we were the only foreigners there. Apart from ourselves we did not glimpse even so much as a cultural attaché.

At the presentation of prizes in the late afternoon the same was true. For once at a ceremony in the capital we did not feel that Korean tradition was flaunting its quaintness before a gallery of foreigners. In the lengthening shadows a quartet of women in blue and white announced in ear-splitting tunes the names of the winners. A small group of court musicians played appropriate music. The successful candidate donned the pale blue coat with the deep blue girdle and the scholar's black hat, and the women shrilled a song of congratulation as he moved forward to receive his prize. The winning poem in each of the two sections was chanted by a young man in the same formal dress.

Then it was all over. But what of the poems? One can scarcely expect the muse to give of her best under such circumstances, and nothing epoch-making was produced. I brought the texts home, and showed them to my learned friends. This is what we made of the Chinese poem:

Among the deeds recorded in our chronicles,
How many loyal men fought in those combats of
  dragons!
We know those invasions rocked the world,
Yet, as we look back, those cataclysms seem empty as
  a dream.
The first supreme commander gained his guerdon at
  the Heron Sea,
The lamentations at the Dragon Gulf reached the old
  palace.
Then it was the Wae robbers, now it is the So bandits.
In what hero can we trust to unify the land of Han?

The Heron Sea and Dragon Gulf refer to the battles of Admiral Yi Sunsin, where he was made supreme commander and where he died in defeating the Japanese. The Wae are the Japanese, So means Soviet, and Han is Korea. But poetry can never be adequately translated, and the merit of this effort lies less in its emotion than in its elegance: 'cataclysms', for instance, is expressed by allusive characters meaning ocean and mulberry trees.

I am not entirely certain what to think of the Paegilchang. It was very pleasant. It was thoroughly alive. It could contribute much to the encouragement of discipline and proper national pride in Korean literature. I hope it will.

Now is the season that my Korean friends most look forward to: the time of clear weather, beautiful trees, and abundant food. The Orient has its spring poems, and Europe has its autumn songs and festivals, but autumn is dearer to the heart of the Korean, while mediaeval lyrics of passionate joy at the coming of spring are more typical of Western appreciation of the seasons. The contrast in the two cultures is clear. Traditionally the Englishman killed off his cattle at Martinmas and resigned himself to live on salted meat until the next spring brought him fresh vegetables, the return of the sunshine and dry weather, fresh meat on his table again.

Korea is entirely different. Quite apart from the fact that the winter gives the farmer a chance to ease off from the heavy field labours of the summer and enjoy some months of so-called leisure, we are now having the best weather, a reduction of summer illness (diarrhoea and other stomach ailments), and a new abundance of food. Visiting my parishioners this week I cannot help contrasting the loaded food-tables with the meagre fare they offered in the spring. The rice bowl is piled high with snowy new rice, and the abundant *kimch'i* includes that delicious confection of young cabbage sprouts in soya sauce, flavoured with pears and ginger and chestnuts, that we have not been tasting for months.

It is a good year for the harvests. The smaller villages are so chock-a-block with rice sheaves that there scarcely seems enough storage space for the grain. The broad plains are closely dotted with stacks and shocks of freshly reaped stalks, ripening in the sunshine. There seems to be rice everywhere: the slopes at the edges of the fields have rows of unthreshed stalks laid out to dry in the sun; even in the crooks of the pine-tree branches there are bundles of rice hanging up to dry. The sun never reached the lower stalks while the rice grew thick in the paddies, and when they were reaped they were still greenish. Now they are gilding in the sunshine and stand in bright relief against the clear electric blue of the sky, which is again reflected in the still puddles among the stubble where the noisy grey-and-white sandpipers are searching for food.

The chief work of the month has been reaping and threshing. Whole families are at work in the field together. In every village of any size at least one threshing machine will be at work in its red-mud, straw-thatched shed, but a great deal of the process is done by the labour of man's hands and arms. A simple revolving drum worked by a treadle threshes the ears on the field, on the road, or in the house yard. And we still have a few foot-driven grain polishing machines, where a group of men combine to work. The men are frequently hired to work for a year. During that year they are fed and clothed; after the harvest they are paid twelve bags of rice.

Michael, my houseboy, is from a different province and is constantly pointing out minor variations in the traditional work habits of the people. He is particularly interested in that we have what is to him a new method of shocking the rice, and our labourers eat fewer meals. He is used to harvesters having each meal trebled, making nine meals a day, with a special name for each meal. Here the custom is less rigid, and six meals or so is more usual. Rice is by no means the whole of the harvest that is giving the countryside its present mellow appearance of abundant goodness. Beside the dry fields there are tall dark shocks of sorghum; and spread out among the graves are the short branches of the cotton plants, ripening in the sun so that the white fluff can burst out from the still-closed pods. In the branches of the nearly leafless jujube trees hang bundles of yellow-stalked, russet-coloured broom-corn, waiting to be turned into next year's house-brushes. In the courts the old women are slitting the red pepper pods with huge scissors, and various kinds of beans are being flailed from their pods.

In the evening the village is pervaded by the pungent but pleasant smell of the field-sesame as the seeds are thrashed from the tiny seedheads. The children carry the seeds in bags or cans or baskets to one of the local 'oil houses' where an old crone presides over a rickety shack filled with a great press and a series of cauldrons. The seeds are boiled and then slowly crushed in the great press. The owner of the press keeps a proportion of the oil, and the rest is taken home. The compacted mass of husks is also the property of the press, except for what the children cadge to chew on the way back. It is a good food for goldfish.

Almost everywhere are chrysanthemums—a few are cultivated but most are the prolific yellow or white wild ones—and what the English call Michaelmas daisies: the starry mauve flowerets that give such charm to the copses. And the village is loud with the rattling clack of cotton-teazing machines, worked by treadles outside many of the cottage doors.

The landscape reacts to the weather to give a different atmosphere to every hour of the day. At dawn the distant peaks rise through the mist with the faintly unreal appearance of paintings on silk. The recent heavy morning dews have given way to a thick hoar-frost that silvers the thatched roofs and lies on the fields like light snow. The midday sun is still warm enough for the ploughboy to work without a shirt, and it combines with the morning frosts to turn the leaves. The oaks are yellowing fast, and here and there a persimmon tree has turned deep crimson, still spangled by the bright orange of ungathered fruit.

The sunset is over all too fast. For a few minutes the smoke rises through a purpled air; then as soon as the sun disappears behind the hills the cold strikes to the bones. The nights, and the occasional days of keen wind, are reminders that winter is very nearly here.

The children have almost spun out their interest in seasonal games: the spinning top, the bowling hoop, the *chegi* —that shuttlecock made of a twist of fringed paper and kicked on the instep, originally weighted with a coin but now more likely to contain a coat button. It is too cool now for five-stones or cat's-cradles out-of-doors.

I am watching for the swallows and the wild geese. They are supposed to change places on the ninth day of the ninth moon. This year we have had a leap moon before the ninth moon, and I wondered whether it would upset the birds' calculations. The swallows should have stayed until the end of October, but they seem to have lost patience, and I have seen none since last week.

My Western prejudice may be reluctant to face the coming winter. The Korean farmer has already begun to look beyond. He was sowing next year's crops nearly a month ago, and already the barley fields can show several inches of fresh green shoots. The blackboard outside the village headman's office is urging us to get the paddies ploughed before the ground freezes, and the shortage of rain is making a few pessimists doubt the quality of next year's wheat. There is no real respite from man's labours or his worries.

Last Sunday afternoon the new protestant church was dedicated at last. It is as handsome as grey concrete can make it, and pleasantly light and airy.

It would ill become a priest nurtured in a great catholic liturgy to comment on the simple, almost informal, service. Except for a few details, it might have happened in any of the world's protestant churches, even to the visiting pastor who had to be prodded into stopping a wordy address which began with the proverbial 'I met a man in the train the other day. . .' I must confess to a strong feeling of distaste at the point where everyone present prays aloud in his own ecstatic words, all at once; especially when, as on this occasion, they are led by a man with a fine sense of dramatic timing who works the hubbub into a crescendo and then as skilfully decreases it again.

Occasions when I come into contact with local churches other than my own always lead me to muse on the state of Christianity in this area. Only very occasionally do my musings make me happy. This time I could not eradicate from my mind the oft-repeated taunt that Christianity, though it is an Oriental religion, is still very much tied up in the ideas of the West or, even more significantly, in the money of the

West. This church, like my own, like another being planned on the other side of the village, was built chiefly from foreign funds. There is a vigorous move to get rid of remaining foreign influences in the leadership of the Korean churches, but so long as there is this high degree of financial dependence, there will remain the distinctively foreign colouring of the thought of Christians. What I see of the Korean countryside leads me to think that this is more of a hindrance to the spread of the Christian gospel than the statistics of the churches might suggest. Foreign relief is still tangled with (and tangling) the state of local Christianity.

It is most discouraging to sit on otherwise completely Korean committees dealing with relief, and sense an atmosphere which is anything but that of the four Gospels. We have no wide-scale blackmarketing in our area, and only one example of the use of relief as part of a proselytizing campaign, but we have a general attitude of mind whereby Christians expect to be receivers of foreign aid, and outsiders believe they receive even more than they actually do. Two causes lie at the bottom of this. One is the general failure of Korean Christianity to have established the idea of the Christian character. Morality has all too often been reduced to a puritanical abstention from wine and tobacco, and Christians in general have not acquired any reputation for a stricter regard for honesty or sincerity than anybody else. The other cause is that to the Korean countryfolk the idea of religion is very closely associated with bodily healings and material welfare. Buddhism and shamanism are both regarded in this way, and I know from experience that pagans will approach the Christian priest when the ordinary shamans have failed. I know also that my catechist woman is referred to by some as 'the Western witch'.

The Christian church has a ministry of healing and a ministry of charitable relief. In our countryside they often take on a disproportionate importance. There is a rivalry between the wandering miracle worker and the lucrative soup kitchen.

The churches are flourishing moderately well. In seeking for reasons one is bound to acknowledge that for the women they provide a most satisfactory kind of super-club, and for many young men Christianity offers the only satisfactory form of mystical satisfaction that they can find. At the same time one must not forget that the Christian doctrine offers the most promising security to the deep spiritual malaise from which most of the people are suffering, though often not suffering consciously.

I meet fairly frequently with clergy and ministers of all the local churches, Catholic and Protestant, for discussions of relief and orphanage work. I also call on them socially. I find most of them sharing my concern, and generally we all admit that our flocks are very similar in both their strengths and their weaknesses.

But there is one point where I, as a foreigner, feel sharply divided from most Korean Christians. That is on the question of Christian unity. The young missionary who comes from Europe, which is alive with a vigorous concern for the reunion of Christendom, receives a great shock in Korea. It has been said that the so-called Ecumenical Movement is the greatest fact of twentieth-century religious history. Yet while in Europe the Roman, Anglican, Reformed, and Orthodox churches are all sharing more and more zeal for healing their schisms, Korea has been tending to further splits. It is not only a matter of the disastrous schisms in the Presbyterian church. It is a question of local churches changing allegiance for the sake of better relief services, and, above all, of the deeply sectarian spirit of the rank-and-file Christians, not excepting my own flock.

It is an unfortunate linguistic development that has made 'Catholic' and 'Christian' mutually incompatible terms in colloquial usage. It is even more tragic that the members of all churches spend so much energy in denigrating other denominations. United committees and councils and so-called union projects in Christian work are not yet dealing with this question at the roots. The fact of sectarianism is accepted and not lamented. Meanwhile here, as elsewhere, the divisions of Christianity weaken its impact on the neighbourhood. The ills that spring from them are a constant hindrance.

Finally, we must admit the intellectual weakness of the Korean churches. In the city I know that this is remarked on by many of my non-Christian friends, Korean and foreign. Even in the countryside I feel the lack of good Christian literature in Korean and the depressing effects of the low level of Christian taste, as expressed in such things as hymns and architecture. In the villages—perhaps especially there, because foreign favour counts for so little—few of the influential or more intelligent men are Christians. And they are by no means country bumpkins.

We missionaries, bound to spend so much time in soliciting funds, fall into a habit of speaking little but good of our work. Korean church leaders catch the habit. The people who stand outside our circles are tempted to think that we are smug. Moreover, it is difficult to point to the weaker points of Korean Christianity without having to confess that the missionaries are largely to blame, and that looks all too much like a readiness to criticize the work of previous generations. But self-criticism, called penitence in the Bible, is fundamental to the Christian life. Our local Christians have applied it to themselves personally, not to their churches as a group.

Yet, turning the coin over, I discover that Christianity has made a tremendous contribution to Korean life, even to life in my corner here. Korea's martyrs are second to none in their glory, and there are many cases of wonderful personal devotion. Moreover, it is of the essence of Christianity that much of its greatest glories shall remain undiscernible to the eyes of the world. Even beneath some of my worries there is a kernel of comfort: it is good if the church is a club, if it satisfies a young man's mystical yearnings, if it draws in the poor and the simple rather than just the noble and the clever. It is right for it to be concerned with relief work and healing, even at the risk of distorting their real values. If these things were quite lacking, we might indeed be worried.

Foreigners are liable to ask me whether I am not discouraged and dissatisfied with what looks to them like a discouraging job. The answer is a simple negative. The history of the Christian church tells of no age when the church was perfect, and realizing the imperfections gives the churchman a good and an immediate aim. Moreover, my conviction remains and grows that Korea needs nothing more than it needs the fulness of the Christian faith. So in preaching to my own flock I constantly try to reinforce and deepen their grasp of the Christian ethic in all its interior profundity, while encouraging them to pray in charity with the members of other churches for the consummation of Christian unity

In England it is also traditionally part of the responsibilities of the country clergy to maintain the intellectual life of the church because they have leisure for study. Oh that I had too!

NOVEMBER

初
寒

THIS WEEK the emphasis of work has shifted from the field to the house. It is true that long piles of unthreshed rice are still snaking across the plains, but the only people to be seen in the fields are the men carrying the remaining grain back to the farmyards. There, on the beaten-earth yard outside the front door, the threshing and winnowing are far from finished, though in one or two places the straw from this year's harvest has already been put on the roof of the house as a bright layer of new yellow thatch.

Intense activity is due in the week when the calendar says 'winter begins' (Iptong)—the work of the women laying down the winter *kimch'i*. The tall Korean cabbage and the long turnip (which might almost as well be described as a giant white radish) are stacked away with salt and water in big crocks in which they will rapidly ferment and ripen into an acceptable side dish.

It is a pity that *kimch'i* has become a joke for foreigners. It is typical of the bad press which Korea has accrued in Western circles since the withdrawal of the Japanese. Quite apart from the fact that *kimch'i* is a very important article in balancing the Korean diet, it is also a food which needs skill if it is to be prepared well, as everyone who has sampled Korean inns will know. *Kimch'i* is also a generic name for a large number of pickles made with different recipes, some of which are admittedly more readily acceptable to the unacclimatized Westerner

143

than others, but some of which are delicious by any standard. I could wish that some foreigners who are fain to blench at the smell of late winter *kimch'i* might understand the feelings that some Koreans have about relatively mild cheeses. Time and again I have found my houseboy destroying perfectly good Western foodstuffs because 'the smell was bad.'

Now the womenfolk are busy blending garlic, pepper, fish, and vegetables into tasty *kimch'i* to last till next spring; and what with all this concentration of activity in the home area, and the seasonal abundance of food, I find it a good time of the year for pastoral visits.

Korean hosts are relentless in their hospitality, and the food provided by a farmer's family in November is more than I can cope with. Even after several miles of cycling over a track that would do justice to a Grand Prix course, I cannot manage more than a quart of rice, especially if a quart of soup goes with it, together with several raw eggs, a plate of persimmons, and the usual side dishes. There is an old and slightly indelicate joke about the English curate who is bound to drink a cup of tea in every house he visits. Korea knows no tea, but just now no house of standing is short of wine, and custom forbids the drinking of an even number of cups. Moreover, the minimum recognized odd number of cups is three. Unless the size of the cups is controllable, one soon learns how many houses can be safely visited in the course of the day.

Part of my trouble is that the Korean village has no place in its life for the swiftly passing caller. Several hours and at least one meal are required for any hospitality to be worth the name, even though the caller lives in the same village. How much more then if he is the priest who has cycled over from the market place?

The welcome is always warm and unfeigned. The people regard it as a reason for compliment if I can remember how to find their houses. I am inclined to think the compliment well earned, for the villages have no streets, and the paths between the villages have no signposts.

Villages must be asked for by their purely Korean names, otherwise you may arrive at a place some miles away from the house you want. Thus I set out recently for a hamlet called in Korean Muddy Field, part of the administrative parish of Fragrant Forest, whose boundaries are long and wide. The whole valley is in fact surrounded by handsome and fragrant pine woods. For finding this particular house it was sufficient to ask where the Christians lived, but generally it is safer to identify a house by the name of the 'master of the door', that is to say, the eldest male member of the family. Alternatively it is often possible to work from the name of one of the youngest members, preferably identifying the house as belonging to some toddler. This method is essential with child informers and generally works best with women.

In Muddy Field I found the youngest member of the family was a little girl, as yet unnamed, and the family, though by no means unlettered, asked me to suggest a name for her. Now this is a very ticklish problem, and the only reason why there is not already a huge literature on it in Western languages is that the use of Chinese characters for names presents one of the world's major problems in practical semantics.

Although most Koreans are nowadays satisfied with one name, this was not always so. Even the most elementary student of Korean history quickly learns not to be exasperated when the same man appears under three or four different names. This week in Seoul I saw men sitting by the roadside who would, for a fee, help you to change or add to your stock of names; but in the country such professional help is not needed. The village seniors (or visitors like the priest) can supply a plenitude of useful appellations.

Many children have milk names. Some of these still have unpleasant or comic meanings to distract the attention of undesirable spirits. Piggie and Dog Dung can be heard in the hamlets, and I am rather fond of a little girl called Crab. More often the milk name is a regular Chinese-style composition which will be changed when the boy grows up and maturer consideration has gone to the creation of a name fit for him to carry in adult life. Even after that the childish name will continue in use among his friends at least until the time of his wedding. This situation is confusing in daily life, and may not even have revealed the name by which the boy is inscribed in the family genealogical tables. My houseboy is more than a little vague as to exactly what name will go down for him in the family tree.

Among the older people this state of affairs causes no concern. Any man of education expects to have a pen-name (*ho*) with a romantic or scholarly tinge to it, as well as a familiar name (*cha*) and an official name (*kwanmyŏng*) for the family tree. For the delight of future historians, the name recorded in the latter document is far from always being the name used for registration in the local government offices. The possibilities are still not exhausted. We have also those who were named under the Japanese regime and changed or half-changed their names after the liberation, as it were on principle.

My parish records become a little complex when a man has more than four names, because our Christians always take a Christian name as well at baptism. The Christian name might be the best way of identifying a man with certainty, if only most Kim would not become John and most Yi would not automatically turn into Paul. Most of the Christian names are biblical, generally based on the Latin version of the original. All have been thoroughly Koreanized, though there are a few Chinese forms. They are adopted on principles which reflect the Western method of choosing names rather than the Oriental method of constructing them. Paul will constantly call his first son Timothy, Philip's brother will be James, and Zachary's eldest is almost certainly John.

For a foreigner to learn to identify country women is even

worse, because so many of them still have no names, at least no names in common use. They must be called by their relationship to their nearest menfolk. I know more than one Korean boy who does not know his mother's name. If you would think to help things out by using their Christian names you will find yourself dazzled by a flock of Marias, Theresas, and Annas with only an occasional Veronica or Agatha.

So one learns very largely to get along without names, calling women 'Auntie' and men 'Uncle' unless their rank earns them a better title. At least we are spared that Western absurdity by which a man is regarded as having only one real name, and anything else is a false alias. In Korea your name is what you are called, and it has no postulated solitary and absolute existence.

This is a bad time for the diary because there is too much else to be done. It is the season for the most intensive visiting of the village flock, and entails periods of days at a time away from the central church. It is also the season of marriages, which are time-absorbing affairs that require a diary entry to themselves. For this morning's writing I will continue and finish the subject which I broached last time: names, and how we use them. It is much on my mind because the grandmother from Muddy Field has been in twice to see if I have thought up a name for her granddaughter. As with the villages, so with some of the women: Korean words have their sounds transliterated into Chinese characters. A girl may give her name as being two characters meaning Establishing Powder, a nonsense whose sound is a simple Korean word for pretty.

Many foreigners are aware of the fact that in most families all the children in one generation share one character-syllable of their given names, so that of their three characters (one being the surname) only one is strictly peculiar to the individual. For most—but not all—families, these generation characters are chosen on the basis of the five elements of the

Chinese cosmogony: fire, earth, metal, water, and wood, in that order, which is the traditional cycle in which the elements are mutually reproductive. There are other families who base their series of generation characters on the *Thousand Character Classic* or the set of astronomical characters called the Ten Heavenly Stems. Few foreigners realize that within a family there is often a sequence between the individual ch racters given to brothers, which may indicate the place of the lad in the family order.

I was recently on a congratulatory visit to a house where a son had been born. He was the second son. While I was there the discussion as to naming him began. An old gentleman present asked the name of the three-year-old elder brother. This boy's personal character turned out to have been the second character from the Chinese classic called the *Book of Changes* (Chuyŏk). The old gentleman was very distressed, because in his opinion the first son should have had the first character of that holy book, and subsequent brothers could have followed on with the rest of the sentence, a character at a time. This is a common practice in older families hereabouts, but this father was a young schoolteacher whose respect for the old customs was ambivalent. The first few characters of the *Book of Changes* are not the only series used for brothers' personal names. Other series include a short list of great Chinese dynasties (Hsia, Yin, Chou), the four mythical beasts (Dragon, Phoenix, Turtle, and Griffin), and the five Cardinal Virtues, or characters whose written forms suggest the ordinal numbers. In another family of my acquaintance, where the generation character is connected with the element of earth, all the boys' personal characters are connected with daylight, and their order reflects the state of the sunlight at different times of the day.

The art of constructing Korean names is fascinating. The harmony of the characters in the names of a well-educated family has a certain beauty of its own. Superstition may also enter in: the practice of counting the number of strokes used in writing a name and ensuring that the total is an auspicious number is not often admitted to, though it is still practised; and the dreams of the mother or father while the child is in the womb may be taken into account. One man I know was called Celestial Flame, because his mother had dreamed of a dazzling brilliance in her breast. Whether this was in fact a presage of future piety was doubtful, because at the age of three he succeeded in burning the house down.

I have said that we minimize the use of names. We have various ways of getting round the problem. Officials like the village headman are called simply by their titles. A man who has a shop or office is called after it; thus we have Post Office Pak, and Dispensary Yu. Members of one's family are called by their relationship, not by their names: Big Brother, Auntie, Little Uncle and so on. In a village where there is only one clan, such as is by no means infrequent in this society where few men leave the village when they marry but all the women do, this leads to a difficulty in the matter of uncles. You cannot call everybody 'uncle', and you cannot distinguish them by their surnames, which are all the same. To call them by their given names would be extremely disrespectful, because they are older than yourself.

The solution is unexpected. You identify them by the place of origin of their wives: Seoul Uncle, Suwŏn Uncle, Anjung Uncle, and the like. Many of the women are called after their native place, such as our Inch'ŏn Auntie and Asan Auntie. So little are the names of women used that people can live in the same house for years and never learn one another's names. I know a high school boy who did not even know his mother's surname until I told him; nor did many other people in the family.

There has been a tabu on certain names, especially those of ancestors. Many men in the villages will still avoid speaking their father's name. If forced to give it, they identify both characters separately so as to avoid pronouncing the name in one breath. This is not so true of the rising generation.

A short while ago I met a striking tabu on names. In the bank there is a framed fascimile of President Rhee's calligraphy, dated on New Year's Day with a character which means dawn, called *tan* in Korean. I was discussing this calligraphy with the chief clerk, who insisted on pronouncing the character as *cho*. There is another character of the same meaning which really is called *cho*; it did me no good to appeal to dictionaries in favour of calling this character *tan*. It had to be called *cho*. Some days later I discovered the reason from a local scholar. The character in question was the personal name (*ŏhwi*) of Yi T'aejo, the first king of the Yi dynasty, and was therefore tabu until the dynasty was over. For some of my villagers the Yi dynasty is apparently still effective! In Seoul this fact is not recognized, and the character is even used on public signs as an abbreviation of another character called *tan*.

And what do the people call me? Most commonly of course, I am just 'the priest' or 'Father'. But when they require a name they use a Sino-Korean one, which looks and sounds like one of their own, and call me Father Ro (only they pronounce it No). The custom of foreigners using Oriental names goes back much farther than late nineteenth-century missionaries. Marco Polo had a Chinese name. From the time of Matteo Ricci onwards, all Roman Catholic missionaries to China and Korea used Chinese names. The first European who lived in Korea, Jan Weltevree, who arrived in 1627, was known as Pak Yŏn. Two things provoked this practice. One was convenience and the fact that non-Chinese names were barbaric to the Oriental; the other was that for writing purposes only Chinese characters were available.

The practice has continued and still has much to commend it. Here in the village such matters as running a banking account, receiving postal orders, and the like are much more easily managed if one has a seal in the normal form. (It would not, however, be impossible without.) The country folk like to have a Korean name for their priest. I suspect that if I had not come here with one, they would have made one, just as the Korean newspapers tend to abbreviate long foreign names like Macmillan and Eisenhower to single syllables, approximating to Korean surnames.

My own Korean name was made up by an old-style scholar in the capital. It bears little relation to the sound of my English name (which is one of those that very few Koreans can pronounce correctly and that cannot be written accurately in Korean script: it always comes out as 'rat' or 'rot'), but is based on its meaning. I am known as No Taeyŏng. I have been interested to discover that Koreans of the clan whose surname I have borrowed are invariably pleased about it. In itself it has gained me at least one very pleasant friendship with the local patriarch of the Kyoha No clan, but unlike some missionaries, I have no sons to be named according to the clan system.

Harmony is important in all aspects of life. It is good to adapt your name to the language you speak. After all, it is what many American families of non-English extraction have done. Jewish people are constantly doing it the world over. Missionaries do it in many countries, and it is by no means peculiar to Korea. Oddly enough, it is rare in Japan. But English is chic in Korea today, and many a high-school boy christens himself in English for smart use. In the village this is rarer, though it is *de rigueur* for self-respecting dogs. The bus driver who lives over at Forge Valley calls his dog Blackie in Korean, but Dispensary Yu has just bought an expensive pointer puppy, and I was asked to name it. Half of Korea's dogs must be called John or Mary or Bess, and they all seemed too hackneyed for this one. We settled for Jim.

All the weddings are not yet over, but I think that the peak season is either with us or just past.

The ordinary way of describing the house where there is a wedding is as a 'banqueting house'. The chief expenditure at a wedding is indeed a matter of food. Of course, a very large sum will have previously been used in the bride's trousseau by her family, but this is accumulated in a more or less leisurely fashion. Farmers are constantly telling me that they have never been better off. There is no doubt that many of them would be better off still if they would moderate their expenditure on weddings, funerals, and ancestral sacrifices, but the urge to make a splash on these occasions is a very deep one, and will not die quickly nor easily.

The advantage of late autumn as a wedding season is that at this time the countryfolk have most ready cash, and food is most plentiful. In many villages there are clubs among the families with unmarried sons or daughters for mutual assistance (to be rendered mostly in kind) when the heavy expenses of a wedding have to be borne.

These country weddings are arranged at very short notice; a couple of months or so is common. In some families the couple are still not allowed to meet before the wedding day, and more often than not they still have no say in the choice of a spouse, chiefly because it never occurs to them that they might gain anything by being fussy. The priest is naturally often called in on the discussion about finding the children's marriage partners. My own reaction to the system, having seen it from as nearly the inside as a foreigner might reasonably hope to get, is that it is no worse than the Western system of marriage by choice and in some respects may be better. The countryfolk have no noticeable anxiety to see the system changed.

When the contract is arranged, the parents on either side often still exchange the horoscopic data of the bride and bridegroom. These consist in the eight Chinese characters called *saju* which specify the year, month, day, and hour of the subject's birth. They are delivered in a plain envelope inserted in a stick cleft lengthwise and trimmed with red and blue silk thread. This is then wrapped in a blue silk kerchief and finally in a kerchief of red silk. Some people go so far as to modernize the custom by writing the date of birth in modern style instead of in the eight Chinese characters.

The age of marriage is generally between eighteen and twenty-five, though not invariably so. There seems to be no particular prejudice as to whether the bride should be older than the groom or younger, but we no longer have child weddings. Last autumn I went to the diamond wedding of a seventy-one-year-old man.

Many weddings are held in church. They have copied some of the customs of a Western wedding and slightly misinterpreted one or two of them. In a village the bride usually wears a borrowed veil with a headdress of tiny shells instead of orange blossom. The dress is invariably of the traditional Korean bodice and skirt pattern, but in white silk. The bouquet may be of artificial flowers and even wrapped in cellophane. The bridesmaid can be relied on to fuss quite unnecessarily. There may also be tiny children, with highly painted faces and wooden expressions, who will stiffly throw coloured paper clippings before the bride and groom as they leave the church.

The bride will in all probability have a chalk-white make-up and look as though she were walking to the gallows. The groom and the priest will scarcely hear her pronounce the marriage vows, because she tries to behave in the Christian ceremony as though she had to obey the rules for silent etiquette among brides in the old tradition. She may even weep if she can manage it. I have a shrewd suspicion that most of these pathetic Korean brides are hugely enjoying themselves. On occasions their stony expression fails to put out the light in their eyes.

Some grooms are terrified, and some are bold. The sensible ones wear a traditional Korean coat, if they have one, but

153

more often they appear in a creased Western suit with a dirty shirt collar turning up at the points. The care of Western clothes is not yet part of the Korean farmers' culture. In any case, both bride and groom will wear white cotton gloves. The priest's major hurdle in the course of a country wedding is not only to get the gloves off, but to prevent them from creeping on again. It is not safe to give them to the bridesmaid or best man. Better put them in your own pocket till the two gold rings are finally in place on the bride's finger.

A few people in the village have 'new-style' weddings, but not many. These are based on the church wedding but are held in some other place and padded out with the interminable speeches which Koreans seem to revel in but most Westerners find boring, even when they can understand them. I know of one case where such a 'new-style' wedding was conducted by a village schoolmaster from the church's ritual, omitting the prayers and the invocation of the Holy Trinity. But even though some of the foreign ceremonies and symbolisms of the foreign style of wedding are not understood by many who follow them (white veils may be worn by widows and pre-wedding mothers), it must be granted that such weddings are generally fairly dignified. The Korean has a passionate love of ritual, but rarely have I seen traditional Korean rites where the ceremonial has been dignified. The rubrics, the motions, are all punctiliously gone through but without any attempt to maintain dignity or create a solemn atmosphere.

At an old-style wedding this is more noticeable. A Christian priest rarely sees an old-style wedding, I suppose. However, this week I went to the wedding of a friend in a nearby village and it was very much in the old style.

I arrived at the bride's house late. Nevertheless the bride-groom had still not arrived. There was an awning over the whole of the house yard. The inner house was crowded with women, all more or less busy with the food tables. All the rooms of the outer house were full of feasting men. In Christian houses I am generally made to sit with the greybeards, out of respect for the cloth, but here I was shown inside to the group of younger men, with whose age I fitted better. They were sitting around, bantering and tightly packed, in the back rooms of the house. One of the younger and chubbier ones went off and dressed up in women's clothes, but he was shy when he had done it, and the venture fell flat.

We had to wait a long time. About four hours, in fact. During most of that time we ate and drank, as well as talked. (I shall always think of talking as the characteristic Korean activity. I enjoy it.) The food was excellent. The two dishes typical of wedding feasts seem to be noodles and *tasik*. The long noodles are auguries of good luck and long life to the bride and bridegroom. The *tasik* are tasty little cakes looking exactly like draughtsmen from a chequer-board. Some are white, mostly glutinous rice; some are tawn, and have a soya base; some are black, sesame-flavoured; but the best are yellow, full of pollen gathered from the pine trees in the spring.

Meanwhile the curiosity of the older men about me was mounting. I was invited, or rather summoned, to the front part of the house. The talk was varied. I had to go through all the usual subjects: English farming, English stockbreeding, English tribal customs, the cost of my fare home, and the reasons why I am not married. We touched on the way to write 'sedan chair' and other recondite concepts in Chinese characters and tried to talk about the controversial new law allowing marriage of agnates. This did not stir any strong feelings because even if it is permitted—and some Seoul people may like to try it on—no one here intends to have anything to do with behaviour which would show such shocking bad form. I was sorry that it did not stir more feeling. It suggested what I often feel: that the farming folk are inclined to regard much of 'what goes in Seoul' as having nothing to do with them. Yet they read the papers and are generally eager to see the country progress.

I have been slightly distressed by some of the comments I have read on this marriage question. The much misused word feudal has been bandied about. In fact the striking thing about Korea is that it is not, and has not been, a feudal country. There has never been the close link between landed gentry and military rights and duties that is essential in feudalism. But feudal has become a word with a bad aura, very useful to those moderns who are liable to attack established custom merely because it is established or because it is not American. Much of Korea's strength lies in its family system, and I fancy that many who would like to crack it open are unwittingly playing into the hands of communism, which hates the family. The modern way of thinking, however, was lost on my farmer friends. They do not see any chance or desirability of the abolition of the old order.

And of course we discussed religion, especially the multiplicity of Christian sects and why they do not unite.

Eventually the bridegroom arrived, by car from a distant town. He also had to be wined and dined. He was temporarily entertained in another house. He was of the timid type and scarcely touched a thing. Meanwhile the boys of the village were collecting outside the house, beginning to tease him, like tiger cubs scenting blood.

At last two of them were allowed in to dress him. He was wearing Korean clothes made of silk with a jade-green waist-coat and a brown coat. He had to wear a blue coat lined with pink, with cranes embroidered on the breast and back. There was the huge, heavy, rigid belt that stands out from the body, and the high black shoes. His hands were covered in long white cuffs. He had a little black veil tied on his head, and the black winged cap stuck on top of it. He looked very unhappy.

The sedan chair was outside waiting for him. So were the boys. As we stepped outside someone drew sooty hands across his face. At once they began beating on the roof of the chair, pelting it with dust and beans. It was carried in a wildly uncomfortable fashion in various wrong directions, especially to toilet sheds, and eventually back to its starting point before finally being taken to the bride's house. Meanwhile the poor lad was crouching inside with his hands over his face in utter misery.

In front went his assistant, a Shakespearean character with one eye who kept protesting volubly in a high voice. He carried the wooden goose, wrapped in a piece of red silk. His face had already been thoroughly blackened by the boys. But he was a professional. He could take it. And give as much as he got.

At the house door the bridegroom stepped out on to a rice bag, and was met by the bride's elder brother, who saluted him by raising his joined hands to his eyebrows. Then the bridegroom was sat down behind a screen until the bride should be ready. His face was wiped clean.

In the middle of the yard was a table set with fruit—especially jujubes, some floating in a big bowl of water—and various kinds of beans, apples, and nuts. There was a red candle and a blue candle. There were two large bottles of wine, one with a pine branch in it and the other with a spray of bamboo. On either side of the table stood a man holding a live white chicken, one of each sex.

Soon the bride appeared, and the groom came out from behind his screen. She was no great beauty, and she looked the less so for her chalky make-up and the circular scarlet spots on her cheeks. Her brilliant scarlet and green dress was good to see, and her tiny crown was beautiful. Until she had made her first deep bow her face was hidden behind the long white silk scarf which she held in front of it with both hands. She was supported by two vociferous old women who kept up a running battle with the groom's old man, directing and correcting the ceremonial.

Then the groom bowed. 'Deeper! Deeper!' shouted the crowd of boys, and some stepped forward to press his head down. The Shakespearean clown belaboured them, and was overpowered by numbers, but he did not stop protesting. Inevitably the groom fell over in trying to get up. 'Do it again!' insisted the boys. In all he did it four times.

Then the bride poured three cups of wine, which were taken to the groom with red and blue threads attached to the cup and saucer. He sipped the first two. At the third one the boys insisted that he drink it all. He refused, and so the youths once again took charge and forced it down his throat. I asked a cheeky young nineteen-year-old husband beside me, 'What happened at your wedding?' He grinned. 'I drank it all straight off.' Then the little dish of *kimch'i* on the table before the bridegroom was seized, and a youth with a pair of chopsticks made of sizable bamboo stalks forcibly fed him with it.

The ceremony was virtually over, but not the horseplay. The groom moved round to the bride's side, and they were draped with paper streamers and sprinkled with paper confetti. Congratulatory speeches were read. Then a whitefaced girl stepped forward to present a wrapped mirror. She held it out. 'Take it, bridegroom!' called the boys. He grasped it through his long silk cuffs, and immediately the girl, with a ridiculously dead-pan expression, withdrew it.

'The greedy thing!' 'Why doesn't he let the bride take it?' and suchlike catcalls came from the crowd. The joke was repeated three times more. Then the throwing of rice and beans and paper began in earnest. Women rushed in to clear the fruit off the table before it flew through the air.

It was too late for the bride to get into the sedan chair to begin her journey to her new home. They would have to spend the night in the village. She was a strong-minded girl, quite unruffled by the horseplay. I was afraid that the poor groom was in for serious punishment all round at bedtime. And he would have further punishment a few days later when he brought his bride back to her home for the ritual visit to her parents.

冬

WINTER

Night covers the mountain village;
  a dog barks in the distance.
I look out of the wicket
  and see only the moon in a cold sky.
What can that dog be doing,
  barking at the moon and the bare hills?

Ch'ŏn'gŭm(17th–18th century?)

DECEMBER

至
寒

WINTER CAME about six o'clock yesterday evening, just as Advent arrived to banish the pleasant pink chrysanthemums—flowers beloved, they tell me, of modest and frugal men—from the altar of my church.

I have been visiting the villages for the harvest thanksgiving services, saying mass at altars surrounded by bags of rice. My travelling is generally in the evening, when the rosy purple light touches the hills with warm colour. The brown leaves of the oaks show like bronze among the dark pines, and the bright green rows of barley shoots stripe the red soil on the slopes. The language is rich in words to describe evening light, and poets dwell more on the atmosphere than on the glory of the sunset itself.

I arrived the other day in a village I rarely visit, just before sundown. The village barber was still trimming heads in front of one of the houses. Most people do not pay him in money. If they do, they give him 100 hwan a time, but they prefer to give him one *mal* of rice and one *mal* of barley every year, in return for the year's barbering.

I went straight in for the evening meal. It was a typical house. In the main room was an old-fashioned cupboard of dark wood with brass fittings. There was an old Japanese wall-clock ticking away and keeping good time. There were piles of bedding and bags of rice. The walls had a medley of paper

coverings, including a large number of calendars distributed by various agencies—political, commercial, and ecclesiastical. Clothes were hanging up in many places. In one corner the low desk-like table of the schoolboy son carried a row of books. The floor-covering was cooked and mellowed to a rich dark red-brown colour by the heating flues beneath.

Over the hottest place lay a sick woman. Her breasts were long since dry, but she suckled a grandchild, a toddler, to keep it quiet. We and other guests who came to chat and to pray all sat in the same room. We enjoyed the view of their fine array of neatly patched socks (even knitted socks are patched with cloth) and the smoke of their long pipes. Apart from the pastoral conversation which was the object of my visit, talk ranged from discussion of the elementary Chinese texts used in the cottage school to questions of taxation and national service. The youths wanted to play chequers.

Everyone was ready for bed by about nine o'clock. I was sent into the little room across the verandah with the eldest son. Normally he shares it with his wife. Here, as usual, the wardrobe is a new one, made of yellow-stained wood and crudely painted glass; there is a long mirror and also a tiny toilet mirror mounted on a set of miniature drawers for the girl's cosmetics. The wallpaper is flowered. The clothes on the wall are covered by an embroidered linen cloth. The ceiling is made of coloured paper, and there is a frame full of snapshots, mostly of people in school or army uniforms.

At the end of a day of village visiting and unremitting talk, I always sink willingly on to the hot floor and am grateful if the pillow is stuffed with beans rather than made of wood. This time it was full of rice husks, which are as good as beans, but the lad wanted to lie awake and talk to me now that he had a chance. He had been reserved earlier on because of his father's presence.

Most of the next day was spent in visiting the houses of the

Christians and trying to avoid eating and drinking too much, but two of the boys managed to get me to the top of the mountain about midday to show off their village. It consists of three separate hamlets nestling in a valley pointing south, half a mile from the sea. Some of the roofs were golden with new thatch and looked charming through the sparse leaves in the autumn sunlight. The hamlets are called Upper Village, Lower Village, and Broad Village, but the children have renamed them Rich House Hollow, Scholar's Hollow, and Stream Dell.

Out there over by the sea is the house of the big sorceress. She is the sort that passes on her powers to an heiress. Her doings are all mixed up with Buddhism, because she was related by marriage to a monk. She has a little shrine, even though it consists of only one paper picture stuck on the wall. She performs her biggest ceremonies there and wears a blue gauze coat, cut like a man's, when she does it. She used to wear a hat, but she does not have one now. You have to pay at least one bag of rice for such a ceremony.

Down here, nearer, in the Lower Village, is the other sorceress's house. The spirit of a little girl who died of small-pox entered into her about five years ago, and ever since she has been a sorceress. She is good at talking with the dead. The boys laughed about all this but refused to take me to see either witch.

In the valley they pointed out their fathers' plots of rice paddy, terraced between the hills. There is not a lot of water in this valley, and the water trickles from the top field through to the bottom. There are always arguments over sharing the water in dry seasons. Once again they explained to me how a dry field is measured in *p'yŏng,* a wet field is measured in *majigi,* and a mountain-side is measured in *chŏngbo;* and what is the average yield of each unit. I find it hard to carry in my head for long any of the complicated figures of Korean computations of land and crops.

Down there, also in the Lower Village, is the cottage where old Kwak the scholar runs the Chinese literature school. You can already hear the singsong recitation of the pupils. There will be more of them later in the winter.

On the other side of the stream is the tiny thatched hut of wattle and daub that shelters a black board commemorating the filial piety of a local girl. No one knows exactly how old it is, but it had lasted at least six generations before it was last repaired—that much is clear from the board itself.

And so the boys talked on, to more detailed and personal notes about the houses and their occupants. We went down the hillside, past an imposing grave of the Min family where the annual sacrifices were offered by deputies from the National Assembly only last week, and in among the trees to continue visiting. The sunshine was still warm. A recently born bull-calf was chasing a cackling hen over the stubble between the houses. The village was full of smiling faces. No wonder Korean court poets developed a nostalgia for rural life. These remote villages still wear the air of an enchanted world. They seemed even more enchanted as I walked over the hills to the next village, so late that it was moonlight.

Much has been written, especially by emancipated young Korean women, about the downtrodden and oppressed life of women in old Korea. Still we hear it said that this is a man's country, that Korean men are selfish, that their womenfolk are depressed and little better than slaves. This is for sure the biggest hoax ever pulled in all Korea's two thousand years of uninterrupted history. If our villages are anything to judge Korean tradition by, and I think they are, then the women have all they want, and they know it. Formal relations and etiquette are one thing: real power is another.

I do not notice that our girls feel any inferiority to the boys. There is disappointment if the first baby is a girl, and when a

son is born you congratulate the father on 'male issue', while for a daughter you speak thankfully of 'an easy birth'. Yet most girls are cherished and loved as warmly as boys, even though a father's references to his daughter rarely swell with pride.

As children the sexes naturally play separately and in groups according to age. Groups of boys start teasing groups of girls very young; but though a sister may have to show deference to a younger brother in public, she will certainly not do so in private, and most girls I know consider the control of their brothers one of their chief functions. A little later on, from shortly before adolescence sets in, the boys become shy and awkward. The girls also become giggly creatures, but often they have more self-confidence than boys. I recall a trio that visited me from a distant village. They were aged about seventeen. The two boys were gangly. The girl was very demure, but she ordered the two boys to kowtow and then conducted the conversation.

Many girls are daunted by the approach of marriage. The cause is less fear of the young husband (if, in modern style, she has met and vetted him, she probably looks forward to that part of marriage) than apprehension at being uprooted and taken away to live in completely new surroundings among people she does not know, for it is still the rule that women almost always go away to a new village on marriage. In the new home she is a person of importance. If she has trouble and unhappiness, it is probably due to her sisters-in-law, who can be vixens. She works in the kitchen a good deal, but she is used to that. In most cases in my experience relations with the mother-in-law vary from happy harmony to the assumption of a domineering attitude by the younger woman. If a baby is conceived early on, the young wife's stock rises and she becomes even more precious to the family.

It is true that the men sit in the front room and call for wine and food and that they eat their meals alone, but women are

rarely happier than when feeding their menfolk and keeping them content, and this need imply no slavery. If the women eat in the kitchen and have their cronies to call on them there and in the back part of the house, it does not mean they are relegated to the scullery. It means they have their own place to themselves, even in a small house, where they can talk at will on matters that interest women and do their sewing on the floor without having the men get in their way. Only the little boys hang around the kitchen door, begging for titbits. Far from being urged into an apron, the men are encouraged to keep out of the way. It is recognized that they do their share of work in the fields.

Father may be head of the family in principle, but mother often has the major say in family decisions. In community affairs she has little part, though she may influence her husband strongly, especially in matters like communal wells. She often controls the purse strings and has a right of absolute veto, which I have seen used emphatically, in the choice of a spouse for a son or daughter.

When she becomes a grandmother her situation eases. She shifts responsibilities and duties on to her daughter-in-law and does less work about the house, even before her strength begins to fail. She often takes up smoking and spends hours with the babies. She mellows into a lovable character, with greater freedom to come and go among the menfolk, even to sit with them in the front room on occasion.

Of course women differ enormously from one another according to breeding and personality but generally Korean women are no blushing violets. Most of the shops down our village street are managed by women. If the police or the war veterans are a nuisance, you send a woman to deal with them. In fact you expect a woman to be tough. I have suffered more invective from Korean women than ever I have from men. But one of the odd things about the Western man is that he is not so susceptible to the female tongue as the Korean is,

because the difference in formal etiquette whereby Western men are more often in female company has a deep effect on both sides. I notice this effect most in the thoroughly unlady-like behaviour of many Korean women in public when they have no men in the party. In buses they have no manners (admittedly no man shows them deference, but they do nothing to earn it); and to see some of them sprawling over the chairs in a restaurant is to have a peep into the manners of the the kitchen where the womenfolk have their meals together.

Of course there are plenty of the other kind: Koreans who are among the most attractive, intelligent, and charming women you could wish to meet, neither flattering nor domi-neering. One or two basic social customs apart, they are not so very different from women anywhere else.

In more ways than one, living in a Korean village enhances my appreciation of what life was like in mediaeval Europe. I used to find the descriptions of the heavy fur robes which the clergy wore in the wintertime rather unrealistic. Now that I have to pray daily in an unheated church I understand tho-roughly. The water freezes in the cruets or becomes ice as soon as it touches the chalice, and the chalice itself burns the fingers into numbness. Even the mind seizes up, and I stumble over familiar words.

The landscape remains true to its nature, and though its beauty changes, it is still beautiful. The fields are so many silvery terraces, studded with the star-shaped tufts of stubble which has not yet been ploughed in. The atmosphere is either clouded with low mist that makes the mountains lovelier, or is crisp enough to make the church bells sound louder than usual. Skeins of wild geese wheel in the sky over the paddies and mud-flats and attract the man with the gun. (As an Englishman I am scandalized by the fact that apparently both Koreans and Americans shoot sitting birds.) The children are well padded, and many of the boys look particularly charming

in their grey pantaloons with a pink shirt and indigo waistcoat. The little wooden sleds, on which they kneel or sit tailorwise, are scudding, propelled by elbow-grease, over every suitable piece of frozen field.

The unusually warm spell we had before Christmas has spoiled some of the ice. Walking through the fields in the morning, I heard it exploding as it cracked under the sunshine. At that time, too, any walking was penitential, because of the mud. Our fieldpaths all carry very heavy foot traffic, and they were soon churned into quagmires that sucked and pulled our rubber shoes off. Then the wind whirled down from Siberia and froze the mud into its churned-up shapes, so that now the tiny ridges cut your feet through the soles of the rubber shoes, and walking has become another kind of penance.

Christmas was a holiday for the whole village, and even non-Christians exchanged a huge volume of Christmas cards, mostly delivered by hand. The Sunday school had shown its annual increment of new members during Advent, and they produced us a concert of songs, sketches, and dancing on Christmas Eve—a spirited and amusing entertainment to which, for the first time in my experience of any village here, everybody listened intently and applauded enthusiastically. Usually one has to call the audience to order from time to time.

The cross above the church was tricked out with fairy lights (we now have a small privately-operated generator in the village which runs from dusk to midnight), and the inside of the church was festooned with coloured streamers and many-sided paper lanterns. Over the altar was a large board with a festal inscription in Chinese characters. There were pine trees too, covered with silver stars. I could not bring myself to ask where the trees had come from, because there are strict laws against deforestation, and it is difficult to cut whole trees in daylight.

Our parish tradition is for the Midnight Mass on Christmas

Eve to be a low one. Many of the youngsters were out till very late singing carols round the village, but it was moving to be in church with a few youths and oldsters, who could easily be transmuted in imagination into the shepherds of Bethlehem, 'while all things were in quiet silence and the night was in the midst of her swift course,' and there on the altar-manger 'Thine Almighty Word, O Lord, leaped down out of Thy royal throne.' But all that is now left of Christmas is the crib by the altar-rail where tiny offerings of ten-hwan notes are still finding their way to the bambino's feet.

The fairly leisured atmosphere of the village has nothing to do with any feast, Korean or Christian, except that the bank has been very irritatingly closed for the first three days of the solar New Year. We are in the period when there is little outside work, and what has to be done at home, such as making rope and mats from straw, is work of no particular urgency.

The schools of Chinese letters are at their peak because the boys have so little else to do. They are cosy, stuffy little hives where master and pupils are only too glad of an excuse to stop work. Then they can doodle on that old Korean version of the slate—a board treated with powdered shells on which you can write with a brush and afterwards wipe the writing off. Like schoolboys in other countries, nearly every boy finds no written word more fascinating to contemplate than his own name and address. Perhaps the teacher will call for 'just one cup of wine' (it always turns out to be a kettleful, and nobody would think of sending any wine back to the kitchen) and relax enough to sing a classical *sijo* or talk a bit about his books and genealogies. But I have little time near Christmas for scholarly dalliance. The whole of my scattered flock wants to see me; I must be off to say mass in far farmhouses, and to visit the Christians, especially the sick.

And now we have school holidays and the children are easier

to gather. In the daytime, when they are not running errands or sledding on the ice, they seem to be playing a great deal of *yut*, which combines the thrills of dice and snakes-and-ladders, using four bevelled sticks instead of dice. It is played in groups and causes the wildest merriment and most frantic excitement.

Frozen hands at the well call forth no complaints from the villagers. Indoors the floor is warm, and the stacked straw grain-bags smell good. There is still plenty of food (although the farmers are very worried about the low price of rice, and their attempts to deal with the situation cause headaches to the bank manager), and there is a whole series of domestic feasts to beguile the time. A few of these are laggardly weddings, but more of them are funerals, or memorial sacrifice days, because it is in this rigorous weather that the old and the sick are most likely to die.

JANUARY

雪

沍

I CANNOT pretend ever to enjoy funerals, and if there is any-thing less pleasant than a funeral on a bare mountain in a bitter Korean winter it can only be a funeral in the English rain; but whereas in European funerals I was always aware of the pomp and the half-hearted evasion of the fact of death that is a legacy of a pre-Christian age, in Korea I am impressed by the way in which the drama of death is exploited to the utter-most. There is no effort to hide its horrors, and there is a strange difference in the behaviour of mourners, a slightly different way of displaying a grief that is really deeply felt.

Our village funerals differ very much one from another in glory. At the bottom of the scale one might put the pathetic group of two or three men who go out at dawn or dusk to bury a dead child, without ceremony, at the foot of the moun-tain. At the other extreme is the elaborate cortege of the village worthy who has merited twenty-four bearers to carry his bier, who is preceded to the mountainside by an army of banners, and whose house is a banqueting-hall and free wineshop for a week afterwards.

Naturally, my immediate experience is entirely of Christian funerals, but these do not seem to differ much from others, except in obvious details. As the sick man sinks, the family begin kneading glutinous rice for the making of wine and rice cakes, and they begin to amass the food for the consolatory visitors. If I am present at the deathbed, we may be able to

173

celebrate the last rites and recite the lovely words of the Commendatio, but with the stopping of the pulse, the recognizably Christian atmosphere falls away at once.

The women's hair is loose before you have chance to see them remove the pins, and the wild and unearthly cry of Korean mourning fills the room. At first, with its deep sobs and protracted wails, it is a terrifying sound. Its effect is contagious, and I have had it bring tears to my own eyes, This keening is a notable feature of the whole funeral procedure. While the body is in the house, the crying breaks out from time to time. At each important point of the ceremony— the binding of the cerecloth, the closing of the coffin, the departure from the house, the lowering into the grave—it breaks out afresh. It is practically reserved to the womenfolk. The men just look strained and depressed. The sons have a formal wailing for greeting guests who come to console them, but younger men will sometimes break out with all the force of the women's crying, and their tears stream without any restraint.

The effect of the sound on other women and girls is interesting. They are sometimes, in spite of themselves, compelled to join in. No amount of sophistication releases our villagers from the urge, and I have seen young women of education deliberately run away from the sound of wailing at a funeral with which they are personally unconnected. They feel themselves getting caught up into its excitement; young girls in their early teens, unrelated to the dead person, will catch the infection and keen themselves into a frenzy at any funeral.

The body is completely wrapped in cloth and bound in seven places before being laid against the wall at the colder end of the living room. A straw mat is leaned against the wall over the body. There is none of the ghoulish English custom of corpse-viewing. In front of the mat, a table bears candles and burning incense and often a picture of the dead person.

There visitors will deposit their gifts of money.

If a parent has died, the sons at once slip one arm out of their coat sleeves and tie the ribbon of the coat under the armpit instead of across the breast. This action, like every other minor point of the ceremonial, is liable to provoke interminable discussion about the minutiae of correct observance. Which arm should it be for a mother, and which for a father?

Many women will come into the house and begin making funeral clothes. Married sons wear complete suits of roughly sewn hemp with high mitre-like hats. Unmarried sons wear hemp veils surrounded by a twist of straw rope and looking oddly Arab. Daughters wear a fillet of straw rope, and daughters-in-law a bridal crown of white paper. Sympathizers—men, that is—may don hempen leggings or tall hempen hats. Most of this dressmaking goes on in the room where the corpse is. No one, except for little children, sleeps until after the burial. Card playing is sometimes used by the men o keep themselves awake. Everyone is exhausted and red-eyed. The stream of guests is continuous, and all are dined and wined. It is a little strange at first to find oneself eating in a room with a corpse at one end, and surrounded by sewing women.

Burial is normally on the third or fifth day (counting the day of death), but Christians frequently have a fourth-day funeral if it is more convenient. The coffin is a plain box, usually made in the house yard. It is small and rectangular. If it is to be buried with the corpse it has the clan, name, and rank of the dead one inscribed down the lid. The body is put in it, generally on the evening before the burial, with a fresh outbreak of wailing.

For the procession to the church or the hillside, the coffin is placed in a bright blue bier with scarlet, green, and yellow decorations. Among these the phoenix (which chances to correspond to an ancient Christian symbol of resurrection) is prominent, and generally on the top of the domed roof is a

gilded lotus blossom containing a red globe. This is clearly a Buddhist symbol, but our villagers are not aware of the fact. Some processions are more impressive than others. The big ones, with the great blue and white canopy flapping over the bier and massed voices of many bearers chanting together as they move with a curious swaying motion, have a barbaric, almost regal splendour. Always there is a hand-bell, rung by a man who generally stands on the bier until it begins to lurch on the hillside. The bell is rung to help the bearers maintain their rhythm. There are frequent stops when the bearers demand more money or more wine. There may also be a drum, and in non-Christian funerals a spirit chair carried before the bier; very occasionally a Buddhist monk is in attendance, telling his beads.

On the mountainside a marquee has been erected with grass mats underneath it. There the bier is set, with the male mourners beside it, while the vistors come to pay their last respects. when they are non-Christians this means the deepest kowtow to the corpse. Meanwhile the grave digging may not yet be completed, especially if the ground is frozen and fires have had to be lit to thaw the top-soil. The grave is dug very wide, but not very deep. The bottom is made quite flat, and then in the bottom a trench is cut which will exactly fit either the coffin or the corpse.

The only women present normally are those attending to the cauldrons for heating rice and soup and wine near the marquee, for on a cold day the men need these things. At a Christian ceremony women will come to the graveside in their white veils.

I was presiding at such a funeral last week on an icy slope. There were fires here and there to warm us. Several of the guests were already getting tipsy. At last all was ready, the gaudy bier was dismantled, the coffin removed and broken open and the cloth-wrapped body carried at knee level by four men up to the grave. It was put in the grave without care

or ceremony; in fact, it had to be pushed and twisted a bit to make it fit the hole. The two sons beside me burst into a roar of grief and a torrent of tears. They quietened while I read the burial prayers and the handfuls of dust were thrown on to the red banner that had been tucked like a coverlet over the corpse. At the end all the Christians joined in singing a triumphant hymn in honour of Christ's resurrection, a strong tune that rode the wind with confidence; but it did not staunch the boys' tears.

We all returned to the marquee and the cooking pots, where the rice was now ready. All protested that they need not, or could not, stay to eat, but most ended by squatting on the hillside and eating white rice and peppery soup. My neighbour was by now quite drunk.

Meanwhile the labourers had covered the corpse with lime, and were beginning to fill in the grave, treading the soil down to a rhythmic song controlled by the beat of a drum. The mourners looked tired out. Well they might be after four unsleeping days of mourning and feasting, of ceremoniously receiving guests and entertaining them.

I find much to approve of in this approach to a funeral. The continual bustle, the realistic treatment of the corpse, the intensive wailing, all seem to have a cathartic effect. The whole performance is dignified, and even has a certain beauty. Unfortunately it also involves an appalling waste of money, and often staggering debts for the mourners.

I would not pretend to estimate the precise importance of ancestral sacrifices in the life of my neighbourhood, but they are still important, and they constitute a severe financial drain on some family resources. Likewise they pose many problems for anyone who is concerned about the development of Korean society.

I had better say straightway that I have never been present at an ancestral sacrifice, though I have heard many accounts

of the ceremony. It takes place at midnight on the day preceding the anniversary of death, and consists of an elaborate ritual meal spread out before the spirit tablet. The senior member of the family ladles rice into a bowl of soup and sticks a pair of chopsticks upright in a bowl of rice. Everyone withdraws while time is allowed for the spirit to come and taste the meal. Then the sacrificers return for the performance of deep ceremonial bows and libations of wine.

There are many books, mostly inexpensive, which give detailed instructions about the size of dishes, the food to be placed in them, and the places they should occupy on the table. These are said to be the kind of rubrics which stimulate lengthy arguments between the participants. I can well believe this because my experience of all Korean domestic ceremonies is that they are ill-prepared, in the sense that there is never any kind of rehearsal, and in the event everyone present has his own ideas of what ought to be done, or else—and this is frequently so with the chief persons present—has a very vague idea of what is expected of him. The result constantly is that a ceremony that stems from an ancient tradition and is the object of tremendous reverence becomes, in its actual performance, a shambles. Often this is true of church ceremonies too, but not always; and where a ceremony is well performed it is by no means always as a direct result of foreign or missionary influence.

Though the ancestral sacrifices are traditionally kept up for three years for a departed father, nowadays many people locally stop after the first anniversary. The annual commemoration of the first ancestor of the clan, or branch of the clan, is kept up for much longer. Heads of houses will travel considerable distances to be present on these occasions. In the case of the No clan, whose name I use in Korean, their venue for the annual sacrifice in honour of the first ancestor used to be at Kyoha just north of the 38th parallel. They now make a longer journey to another clan tomb-site in the southern

province of Chŏlla.

It is difficult to arrive at a just appreciation of the religious significance of these rites. All Christian churches in Korea forbid their members to have anything at all to do with them; but it is a mistake to expect from Oriental religious systems the kind of dogmatic theological explanation of rites which Western religious systems can always offer with regard to their own services. This partly explains why the early Jesuit missionaries in China allowed their converts to continue with the sacrifices, and why that distinguished Korean protestant, Pyŏn Yŏngt'ae, has been able to hold a view of the matter in direct opposition to the official protestant attitude. In themselves, I do not believe that the ancestral sacrifices have any profoundly religious significance for those who perform them. The speeches made to the spirits are more rhetorical than prayerful. The most potent motives for the continuance of the practice are social: the strong Korean reluctance to break a tradition, and sense of loyalty to the family group. Of course, the religious aspect comes to the fore in confrontation with Christianity. Many men who have to all intents and purposes accepted the Christian faith, and whose families have been baptized, never become church members because their family duty at the sacrifices would come into conflict with ecclesiastical regulations. In our district, women do not take part in the sacrifices, so they never face this dilemma.

Women do, however, perform the less formal sacrifices at graves connected with the moon festivals, where they give themselves up to a frenzy of weeping and wailing. And they may set out the food daily in front of the spirit throne if one is kept in the house for a period after a death.

This week I attended an interesting village memorial ceremony. It was not a Christian service, but Christians took part, because the dead man had been a Christian who was also a benefactor of the community at large. The middle-school hall

had a photograph of the dead man, swathed in black and surrounded by Western-style funeral wreaths, on the little stage. There were also candles and an incense burner. The ceremony was simple and dignified: after a long eulogy of the deceased, representatives of various groups of people read memorial speeches, most of which apostrophised the dead man. The mourners were present again, in hempen mourning clothes. The male mourners approached the dais one at a time and burned a little incense. (It was in the form of green joss-sticks.) Then all the dignitaries present and representatives of each corporate group did the same. With that, all was over. It had not been a sacrifice, it had not been explicitly a religious service. Yet inevitably there had been a religious atmosphere.

Naturally I had celebrated a requiem mass that morning. Our Christians' piety toward their dead keeps my black vestments in constant use; and by a touching symbolism that the villagers may not appreciate, it is common for the humble families to make the customary offering in the form of candles—a promise of light to come.

In connection with the same celebration I went in the evening with a group of the faithful to have a service in the dead man's house. It was full of bustle and noise and the entertainment of guests, as though it had been the funeral day itself, all over again. Beggars had come from far and wide to live off this unbridled hospitality. The waste of money was appalling. Like everyone else, I too was constrained to eat and drink before leaving. Before I got up, a tired son of the departed (he is a well-educated army officer) asked about English customs at death anniversaries. On hearing that there was no wholesale entertaining, he sighed and said, 'The sooner we get rid of this Korean custom, the better.' I understood his fatigue, his conscience about the waste of money that does so much to ravage the Korean rural economy; but I wonder what Korea can find to replace the present system of honouring her dead which will prove as effective in knitting her strong family

system. Or must Korea undergo some more radical change in her basic community structure?

I never cease to wonder at the blue quality of Korean daylight. The snow intensifies it. The last heavy fall has covered the whole countryside with a dazzling decoration as though it were the soft sugar frosting on a cake, and the blue light is reflected even from the shadows, so that sunglasses were never more useful in the summertime than they are now.

The houses have taken on a second roofing, a heavy blanket of snow, and all the eaves have foot-long icicles which break and fall with a delicious tinkling sound as the children smash them by running a stick along the row. There are soft white tufts and bunches of snow in the sombre green of the pine needles, and their prettiness mocks the pathetic scraps of cotton wool that we put on our indoor trees at Christmas time. The deciduous trees, with their tracery of leafless twigs turned into a sparkling vision of fairyland by their coating of frost and snowflakes, and the oaks still sporting their russet foliage, are even more beautiful.

It is a clean, crystal beauty, lovely but cold. The breeze has made many miniature curling drifts along the tops of the furrows in the fallow fields, as though some superb confectioner had been at work with his icing tube. And here and there the barley spears prick through the surface. The fields look clean, and work is impossible. True, the streams still flow under their ice, and there are places where holes can be cut and the fish caught and lifted through them, but the inlets of the sea are a forlorn and miserable sight. The rapid tides constantly move away from beneath the ice, which collapses in jagged pieces into the mud beneath, so that at low tide the estuaries are covered with dirty broken floes. The fisherfolk can no longer bring their boats up to the inland hamlets.

Women, of course, must still work on, staggering from the well with heavy yoke-loads of water, cooking in a smoky

kitchen. They come to the door, wiping their swollen red fingers on a corner of the apron or pushing back their straying hair with the back of a hard-worked hand. Meanwhile the men take life more easily, working indoors at straw or reed weaving in the daytime, venturing afield very little except on market day, spending the evening with cards or chequers or conversation.

Now is a good time for riddles and playing with words. There is a couplet of balanced Chinese characters attributed to the vagabond poet Kim Sakkat that says: 'It hovers in the air like butterflies, it croaks under foot like frogs.' (The answer, of course, is the snow itself.) And at this time of year grandfather chants under his breath as he reads over the tattered and dog-eared yellow books that are normally shut away among the seedbags and the empty pots in the cupboard in the wall. He sways as he sings and has a continual incendiary battle with his long bamboo pipe. Sometimes when I call, I find him surreptitiously pushing a brightly coloured monthly magazine, with a pretty girl on the outside and not-so-improving material inside, away out of sight under his hams. There are limits beyond which a Confucian gentleman cannot pass in public, but in private he can relax. It is a good time of year indeed to sit in a warm house and read and wait for the food table to be brought in at regular intervals, a time when the old man can be least aware of the changing times, save for the fact that sons and grandsons are no longer devoting so much time to Chinese studies are they used to do.

FEBRUARY

I ENJOY READING accounts of Korean life of fifty or sixty years ago and comparing them to the present state of the villages. J. R. Moose wrote his *Village Life in Korea* in 1909, with the Ch'unch'ŏn area of Kangwŏn-do in mind. J. S. Gale's *Korean Sketches* are ten years older, and there are other books too. Some of them are written in a highly romantic vein, their tone varying between a delight in the exotic and a sharp criticism of the country as 'undeveloped'. They are all still far too much in use as source-books for writing about contemporary Korean life. This is partly justified: reading them in my village house I am frequently subject to the thought 'plus ça change, plus c'est la même chose.' In some ways it does not change at all, or only the name changes. The pedlars' guilds represented a factor in society that has been replaced by other groups, with less picturesque names such as 'veterans society', but the same practices.

The normal course of justice is scarcely more respected in its new dress than in its old, because although there is no dealing out of corporal punishments at the county seat, the officer of the law is still treated as a bogey. This is most unfair to our village policemen, who are gentle and courteous fellows; and when questioned closely on the subject, my parishioners admit that their attitude to the police is still their old attitude to the Japanese regime.

Most of the local rites are scarcely changed: funerals, wed-

dings, sacrifices, all continue. What have we that marks our progress in half a century? We have lost the topknot and—except in a few hamlets—we have lost the *yangban*, the old-style aristocrat, though there are still villages where the old *yangban* family assumes dictatorial powers. There is no longer any stabling for ponies at the village inns, and the old books are full of pony stories. Above all, we have lost the fleas. Once only in Korea have I slept with fleas. That was on a proper bed in a house in the city of Taegu. In 1900 fleas occurred in every chapter of a Korean book: where have they gone, and why?

What we have obviously gained is banking, buses, and schools, and these have changed the heart of the village more than its appearance. But what of the hamlets? There are still many where even these things have little impact. Men go to the army and return, apparently to live contentedly on farms where they use thousand-year-old tools and think as little of the strange doings of politicians and city-dwellers as their predecessors did generations ago.

Seoul is the great wen where life is not quite normal, reached by adventure and the discomforts of bus and train, but instead of gaping at the palace gate we nowadays tremble on the threshold of department stores and return home forgetting all but the few gewgaws we bought there. Yet all our country-dwellers are by no means the same. Some may aspire to Seoul standards; the majority are content to leave Seoul in the realm of El Dorado: a place where a fortune (or at least a living) can be had for the asking, should life in the village ever become quite impossible.

The dominant feature of the month has been lunar New Year's day. A visitor from the nearest city, Suwŏn, tells me that many of the children there knew nothing about it, but in our village it is, together with Ch'usŏk, one of the two really big holidays in the year. Only on these two occasions do the shopkeepers board up their fronts and refuse to trade. Only

on these two days can you guarantee to see a lot of traditional festive clothing.

As usual, the feast really began at the specially augmented market that preceded the actual day. We are still far from thawed out, and there was mud inches thick on top of hard-caked snow and ice in all the lanes. The low awnings to catch the drip from the roofs made walking difficult, but the market was gay as ever. Rolls of flowered silk for women's clothes, new outfits for the children, brocade waistcoats for the menfolk were piled perilously near the sticky mud. There were several black-pepper grinders, and a troupe of performers with a loudspeaker, selling medicines. The village was crowded. Not everybody had come to buy: some, who were not really there for the market at all, had come just to stare.

I found old Kwak, the Chinese teacher from that village two hours away, contentedly filling his pipe in one of those shops that sell bootlaces and soap and barley sugar, candles and string and wallpaper. He had just come for a spree and was about to wade back home through the mud. The air rang with greetings—'No Sobang, I haven't seen you for months!' said a man whose face I did not recognize—the calls of the vendors, the sound of the gongs with which they tried to attract attention, and the chatter of the crowds and the children. All was muddy and cold, but very jolly. A drunken man with a roll of pink silk under his arm greeted me warmly. A begging war-veteran slipped and fell in the mud and then wiped his hands on the stockings at a nearby stall. The merchants of sugar cakes and puffed rice were doing a great trade, and the bunches of squids lay clammy and glass-eyed on the fishmen's boards.

The inside of the post office is always dark on market day because of the clothes-sellers' stalls which cover up the windows. I found the postmaster and his staff taking their ease. There was one question which had been troubling the whole village: which day was really to be New Year's Day?

All the old books had it for Tuesday, but the Central Observatory said the new moon would not be in conjunction with the sun until eight minutes past midnight, on Wednesday.

The village police chief had already invited me to take a glass of wine at his house on Wednesday. The schoolmaster insisted on sticking to Tuesday, tradition being superior to astronomy. The postmaster cannot shut his office at all for lunar festivals; he said, 'Only the President and I keep the law about the calendar.' This is one point where country life is awkwardly poised between the old order and the new. The effective calendar in the farmer's life is the lunar one. There are still a great many moon festivals, and the lunar new year is much more important than the solar new year, even for schools. All printed calendars need to show both systems, and I have to warn all the outlying villages of my visits by supplying two dates.

Our fifth-day markets are the only events fixed according to the days of the Western months of the sun calendar. Even so, we switch our market days about if they are likely to interfere with any notable lunar festival. Salaries are paid on the twenty-fifth of the solar month. We ought to give our birthdays according to the sun, but many of the villagers know them only according to the moon. (This is, of course, essential for the purposes of the fortune-teller.) We cannot truly be said to follow either one calendar or the other. We keep them both, but our village still has a strong penchant for the lunar system.

Most of us stuck with tradition and kept New Year's day on Tuesday. We all conscientiously added one year to our age and agreed that the Year of the Dog had really begun. I have not grasped all the fulness of the meanings of the year animals as they are applied horoscopically, but they are a frequent subject of amiable banter. You are frequently asked in the hamlets not 'How old are you?' but 'What is your birth year?' When I answer 'The Year of the Ox,' there is always a laugh,

because the ox is born to hard labour. I miss some of this sad fate because my birthday is in the seventh moon, when the oxen are having a rest before the harvest.

The Korean almanac, with its complex columns of Chinese characters and its very full astronomical data, is a fascinating affair. I like the two clauses—practically untranslatable—that stand at the head of each year in the perpetual calendar. One says (for this year) 'Sin comes on the 6th.' This means that the character sin occurs for the first time this year in the sixth day of the year. The period between New Year's Day and the first sin day was reckoned to be equivalent to the period during which the rice flowers would be open in that year. Generally speaking, the longer it is, the worse it is for the crop. Three days is ideal. Six is not too bad but nothing special. It could be eleven or twelve. The parallel clause says: 'Three dragons rule the waters.' This means that the astrological character for the dragon occurs first on the third day of the year. The higher the figure, the more dragon spirits will be active in sending rain. There should not be much rain this year, because the maximum number of dragons is also twelve.

There are other ways of foretelling the year's weather too. One year's eleventh moon corresponds to next year's fifth, and the twelfth to next year's sixth. Much snow in a winter moon predicts much rain in the corresponding summer moon. The twelfth moon has been snowy, so next sixth moon should be very wet. (That means July, and I feel reasonably sure of the prophecy, because the monsoon season scarcely ever misses that month.) But not many are bothered by such details on New Year's Day: for grown-ups it is a time of feasting, of visiting graves, of giving children a good time.

We began the day with a sung requiem mass. Then came the first party: a breakfast party. The distinctive food is a soup made with tough white rice-dough rolled into sausage shapes and then cut into slices and cooked in broth.

187

Even before breakfast the business of the New Year bows was started. The children come one by one before their elders to perform a deep and solemn kowtow. Some do it gracefully, and others do it with an engaging lack of balance. The boys kneel and put their foreheads to the floor; the girls sink to a sitting position without bending their backs on the way down, and then bow. Of course this display of congratulatory reverence deserves rewarding. Cakes, sweets, cash—all are acceptable. Having revered your parents and been duly rewarded you can start thinking of other people who are susceptible to this kind of flattering. What about the foreign parish priest? So in they come, Christian or not, small fists crammed with 10-hwan notes already earned. 'Please sit down properly, Father, and receive our New Year bow.' Having received some sixty bows or more by the end of the day, I felt quite a connoisseur of their performances.

So out to the proper games of the day. There was much throwing of *yut* sticks, that Korean variation of dicing; and the girls in their golden bodices and scarlet skirts jumped to dangerous heights on a seesaw, while little brother sat in the middle of it to hold the board firm. There were a few kites too, unpretentious white paper-and-bamboo ones giving great joy to the little boys who had flying contests with them. But we no longer cut kites loose to bear away our ills on the first full moon of the year, and even moon-viewing on that day has much declined. Lunar New Year has become a day for gorging and rest, and for the pleasure of the children.

At this time too the voluntary fire brigade will get out the musical instruments of the farmers' band and go round the village with a tall bamboo pole covered with white cloth and paper fringes and bobbles. They play and dance before each house and receive contributions in the form of a sacrificial offering which is variably said to go towards the expenses of the 'Brigade of the Valiant and Righteous' firemen or to renewing the musical instruments. Some sort of spirit is vague-

ly felt to live in the fetish pole, and the houses get some general blessing from this experience. It is equivalent to the *kosa* performed by the wandering dancers. Even those concerned in the performance are vague about the theology of it.

There is a general feeling that the celebration of New Year is a dying thing. It seems less virile than Ch'usŏk, because the lunar New Year has not the vital significance of the harvest, and the memory of the dead is less on our minds than death itself is in the winter time. In fact, on New Year's Day I had to go over the muddy hills and take a funeral.

Books about Korea always give some space in their section on religion to 'shamanism and animism'. Frequently the two things are bracketed together as though they were indistinguishable, and more often than not the writer suggests that both are dead or dying forces in rural Korea. So far as my corner of the land is concerned we can distinguish between them fairly clearly, and neither is by any means dead. Shamanism is the more spectacular and undoubtedly more pernicious from a social as well as from a religious viewpoint. We have far more shamans, sorceresses (*mudang*) and male witch doctors (*pansu*), than we have either Christian ministers or Buddhist clergy in our county, and they have a much larger clientele, especially in cases of sickness. They will ensure blessings as well as exorcise evils.

A few months ago Michael, my houseboy, rented a room in the village and found a decaying fish head nailed to a pillar inside. The landlord was as insistent that the revolting charm must stay where the sorceress had put it as the boy was that it should come down. It was but one of several different kinds of nests for spirits, made variously of paper, selvedges, or other rubbish, which the witches will instal in a house.

Not long after, an old scholar told me mournfully that a very charming red-gate memorial had been razed over at Such'on village. Apparently the family to which the memorial

belonged had an illness in it which did not respond to the usual sorcery. The witch had finally declared that the memorial must be pulled down. Now this memorial is essentially a good thing, an honour and a blessing to the family, so my old friend thought the witch was displaying abysmal ignorance by prescribing such measures. But, he said, it shows how powerful is the hold of the witches over the people when they can be obeyed even in such insults to family honour.

The thought of the sorceress gives everyone—even the most enlightened young man—a *frisson* which is not entirely unpleasurable. She is socially ostracized, together with her family. Her house is set apart, and people do not mix in its society. Her religion is quite without constructive elements, a compound of profiting by the sense of the numinous in simple people and playing on their fear. This is perhaps the one feature of Korean country life which I would most willingly see disappear, even while I respect the forces which bring it into being.

Animism is slightly different, though the witch may dabble in it. Under this heading one must presumably class the various superstitious habits which are individual or family performances. These include such things as the scattering of hulled rice in the yard as an offering to certain spirits, often not clearly identified, and the setting forth of rice cakes and bean confections on irrigation dykes or near to particular rocks and trees. In one or two places we have cairns set by the path outside the village and often at crossroads. They are never by motor roads. Passers-by throw a stone or a broken pine branch on the pile. It grows imperceptibly, because not many now add to it. By one of them stands a magnificent old tree. When I last went that way a pathetic little piece of pink-and-white rag was fluttering in one of the lower branches, the embodiment of some heartfelt prayer. I have often found the silver-heart ex-votos and crutches in Christian churches pathetic enough, but at least they represent thanks for favours

received and not a fumbling magic for averting or diminishing disasters.

It is difficult to know in how many of the house gardens there are those conical piles of straw thatch which are believed to guarantee blessings and wealth for the household. One rarely sees them because the fence of sorghum stalks or the thick mud-wall effectively makes all these gardens secret ones, and visitors are almost never invited to look behind the house. I did once, however, see such an object destroyed by an old catechist in the garden of a lapsed Christian. It contained a covered earthenware bowl of unhulled rice and a large live rat (which had no part in the magic). Another was quite empty. Sometimes similar straw cones are erected by a village in a grove of trees on the crest of a small rise. Individuals occasionally make food offerings by them, but I have never heard of any public function there.

It is quite a different matter at the village shrines of the so-called Mountain Spirit, who is really the tutelary god of the place. These are easy to see, and the main road south from Seoul has a fair sprinkling of them on either side readily visible from the bus or car, once you have picked up the habit of looking in the right places. They are quite small, rarely as much as six feet square in floor area. Most of them are built of wattle and daub and have a heavily thatched roof. I know one of brick and many of straw. Almost without exception there is a grove of trees around the back of the shrine. If there is no grove when the shrine is erected, one is planted. The shrine stands on a hilltop. The inside is variable. The best kind, like the one in my own village, has a painting of the Mountain Spirit, generally veiled with red gauze. He is shown as an old gentleman with a tiger. Often he has writing brushes beside him, and sometimes—always, if he is near a Buddhist monastery—he holds a lotus flower à la Bunthorne.

Sometimes the shrine does not belong to a village but is known as a mountain shrine. Then the picture is more likely

to be of tigers only. I know one remote mountain-top over-looking the gulf, where two splendid red-mouthed tigers snarl on the wall. They are a ready symbol of the fierce Mountain Spirit. In this shrine there is a wooden tablet below the picture, made like a spirit tablet. On it is pasted a piece of paper with some neatly written Chinese characters. They appear to be a triple invocation, each phrase beginning with a Sanskrit word, and illustrate another aspect of Korean Buddhism's implication with animism. I have checked it in a common book of Buddhist prayers and charms. It seems to mean:

Great Spirit, King of the Mountain,
Hail Thou That Dwellest Forever in This Shrine!
Great Spirit, King of the Mountain,
Hail Most Excellent in All Virtues, Utterly at Peace!
Great Spirit, King of the Mountain,
Hail, in All Directions of the Universe, Most Spiritual,
Most Holy!

But it is obscure. Certainly it is not the Chinese of the orthodox classics, and none of the local scholars can give me an authoritative interpretation.

Many a shrine has no picture. Near the coast, where the shrines seem commoner, they sometimes have the ceiling covered with hanging pieces of blank white paper. The fisherfolk are often unlettered, and their life makes them very aware of the need for prayers and grace. On the little altar-shelf, even in the pictureless shrines, there are infrequent offerings of rice wine or dried fish and very rarely of a 10-hwan note (the smallest piece of change we have), which represent the small amount of individual worship offered in these places.

The village shrines generally have an annual sacrifice on a large scale at the end of the year. Almost every non-Christian household in the village contributes towards the annual restoration of the building and the provision of the sacrificial

food. The list of subscribers is pasted on the wall inside. The service takes place after dark by the light of flares, with much clanging of gongs, on a day chosen because it is deemed propitious. There is no priesthood. Some old man of standing chants the prayers, which are highly Chinese compositions and next to unintelligible to the people attending. I once questioned the worshippers on the fringe of the crowd about it, and they were ignorant even of the existence of the picture in the shrine.

Our village shrine is maintained by the family of the man who first erected it some fifty years ago. I met the present incumbent once. He told me that he does not believe that there is any virtue in the shrine worship, but he cannot bring himself to break the family tradition of caring for it. Indeed, he told me that the Japanese police had once moved the shrine and cut down the great tree which stood by it. The villagers warned the Japanese, but they persisted. The work was half done when the police chief's little son died. But still the work went on. Sure enough, his other son died when the work was completed. The whole village has never forgotten the story.

The shrine is the pagan parish church. When there is any dancing in the village there is always some in front of the shrine. The spirit is the tutelary deity of the farmers and the fire brigade. In this sense he has at least a small social role, but it is not much, and some of the villages are not now keeping up their shrines very well. Nevertheless, I suspect that a bad year or a calamity might see them restored.

Last of all there are the famous so-called devil-posts. They really represent cosmic gods. We have a pair in one village in our area, about four feet high, crude, and green with age. When I last saw them they had paper fillets bound round their heads. Sacrifices are made to them but beliefs about them are very vague. On the other hand, I have a belief about those which appear brand new by the main roads. I believe their object is the American camera tour.

周
丰

THE
RETURNING
YEAR

White snow still covers the earth,
the mountains gleam like pale jade;
Plum blossom is half-open,
bamboo buds are bursting green—
Come my lad, fill the cup to the brim,
the Spring feeling is on us!

Anonymous

MARCH

仲
春

EVERY YEAR the seasons repeat their pleasures, expected and yet always with the freshness of a surprise. And every week I discover some fresh facet of our village life or some fresh experience in a familiar situation that makes monotony impossible.

First the ever-fresh signs of spring. The herons are here, reconnoitring the paddies. The spruce little drake, all pearly grey with a sleek green head for his courting wear, is busily swimming at the head of his miniature harem across the flooded paddies—just messing about, chatting. The mauve-pink azaleas are out and some of the golden forsythia. Under a bank here and there is a tiny clump of violets—they are called 'barbarian flowers' here, and they are disappointingly scentless. Out on the windy slopes is the grandmother flower, a deep-maroon anemone, with its hairy grey-backed petals. The frogs are beginning to call, and the larks rise high in the morning sky. It is time to be about and start work.

We have planted our young trees. Even the churchyard has received a new batch of little pines and a few hibiscus; and now work is beginning on the rice paddies. First of all the baulks are rebuilt with mud from the edges of the fields. This is no joke for the casual passer-by, because six inches of fine grey mud is a most unsatisfactory surface for a narrow path between two flooded paddies. Often it takes a long detour to find a dry path. Then the paddy is ploughed by patient beasts

and men, who were this week working knee deep in icy-cold water. Meanwhile fine mud is being patted and pegged into the rectangular beds that will take the rice seed later on. Men begin to feel busy, and the landscape is animated again.

Tradesmen, of course, unless they also farm land, scarcely feel this rhythm. It is a slack time for the village photographers, of whom there are four, to my knowledge. Autumn weddings give them their peak work season.

This week I visited the oldest-established of the four. The studio has a beaten-earth floor; at one end is a scenic panel, painted mostly in sepia. The lighting comes from the generous window space, a glass plate in the roof, and some white paper reflectors. There is a cloth-covered table with a bunch of paper flowers in a vase, and a couple of stools. It is all operated now by the fourth son of the family of twelve, who is nearly of military age. He led us into his processing room, a minute space between two buildings, with big gaps in the floor and a piece of blanket to serve as both door and wall at one end. We clambered over some *kimch'i* pots and an old fire-place to get up into the dark room. Across one end was a shelf with a tiny square orange-glass window above it.

He offered to demonstrate his technique. A young brother was hailed who brought a bottle of water, certainly not distilled. Two kinds of chemicals, both identified by English initials meaningless to me, were measured out by guess-work and shot into the water. The bottle was shaken, and the liquid poured off into a none-too-clean tray. A battered cardboard box yielded various kinds of printing paper, which were folded and torn to the size required and set in a frame with the negative. Then the orange glass in the window was slid back with a crash and the frame was uncovered. This was repeated. Then the paper was put in the tray of liquid. To my great surprise a fair picture appeared.

But the young man was dissatisfied and decided that the face of the figure in the picture needed extra printing. This was

achieved next time by exposing the negative and printing paper once to the uncovered window, then hiding their lower half under the shelf for a second exposure. The result was an improvement. The whole process was achieved with a tremendously efficient sounding series of cracks of the frame on the shelf and the window in its slot, and with great speed. My knowledge of photography comes from books with tables full of decimal points, arcana which I have never dared to profane. But, oh yes, our young friend can deal with fine-grain prints too—and doubtless all very profitably at high speed above the *kimch'i* pots.

The barber's shops (there are three of them) have a different rhythm. It is slow and gentle. The youth of the village congregates there with newspapers or a portable radio. This week I had my hair trimmed to the accompaniment of a selection of American songs and orchestral pieces. The mirror in front of me showed thatched houses, and hens pecking about in the village street. One had that quaint sensation of living in the midst of a documentary film. Then the programme changed, and the modern music gave way to an old Korean form of popular entertainment, a long musical folk-tale called 'Paebaengi's Seance'. The pipe and drum, the falsetto male singing, the inconsequent cadences do not appeal to the modern ear. A youth leaped forward to the wireless set. Ah, I thought, we do not care for this old stuff. But no, he was readjusting the tone, and did so again several times before he was satisfied that the programme could be properly relished.

It was still going on when I left the shop, and as I passed the Forest of Books (the newspaper shop) I saw a group of schoolboys clustered around another wireless. I was hailed to stop and listen. Paebaengi's doings are highly regarded. They tell of the antics and tricks of a bogus young male witch; but other things than songs remind me regularly of the doings of sorcerers. A youth appeared at church last Saturday hoping to

get his head cured of its giddy sickness. A blind herb doctor had given him medicine and two identical *pujŏk* to carry in his pocket. The *pujŏk* were little oblongs of paper with occult patterns, remotely like seal impressions, drawn on them in red; but they had not worked. He slept one night with us and felt much better; no doubt a quiet night in a ventilated room had been helpful.

I was reminded of the houseboy of some American Air Force doctors. They had signally failed to cure a swelling of his right eyelid. Finally he had consulted a wise woman, who had given him a string to tie round his left big toe, and certain other rites to perform which he would not divulge. The next morning the swelling was gone. The doctors lost much face, and the boy is preserving the string against further emergencies.

Sickness also made its periodic appearance with poor mad Agnes, who is having another spate of her mania and can be seen being chased about the village by shouting children, while she hurls bloodcurdling threats back at them. The other morning she burst into church while I was saying mass, but once inside she quietened down and restricted herself to singing a few unearthly hymns. At least she goes to the church in her distress, and at least its atmosphere is calm. To that extent it is better than the witches and cairns and mountain shrines.

APRIL

季
春

So EASTER is here again. This year there was a coincidence between the church's calendar and the Korean calendar which half wrote the Easter sermon. The Christian feast coincided with Hansik, Cold Food Day, an ancient commemoration from China that honours a man known to the Koreans as Kae-ja-ch'u, a faithful servant of Duke Wen of the Chin (or Tsin) dynasty of the seventh century BC. After sharing his prince's exile for nineteen years, he finally declined to accept any reward or further public office when the prince resumed power. To avoid royal pressure he hid in a mountain forest with his mother. Legend says that the prince fired the forest to force him to come out, but he and his mother preferred to perish in the flames. In memory of this event, it is said, the North Chinese and Koreans kept a Feast of No Fire, and so had to eat cold food.

There was a Korean custom of eating special dough cakes made with azalea flowers on this day, but it is more important as the day when family graves are visited and repaired after the winter frosts. I am told it is also the most appropriate day for moving graves if that is considered desirable for geomantic reasons. This is still sometimes done in our district.

The day is computed as being one hundred and five days after Tongji, the winter solstice. It therefore always falls in the first week of April. One proverb says that if it falls in the second lunar month the flowers are in bloom, but if in the third,

they are not. This year it was in the second, but there were very few flowers.

An old Christian discussing this coincidence with me asked how Easter was calculated. I had to refer to my library before I could give the correct and accurate answer: it is the Sunday after the first lunar fifteenth day after Ch'unbun (that is the first full moon after the spring equinox).

This year's paschal full moon was on Monday night. The next day it was again shining brilliantly, and as I came out of church after a service on Good Friday evening, I heard the rhythmic singing, drumming, and thuds of men preparing a house site. This work is nearly always done in the late evening by moonlight, when the men can gather for it after their necessary daylight field work. I decided to stroll down the road and watch them for a little. I was not expecting to find them preparing a site on part of my church property. I wish I could say I had been more surprised, but there are doubtless good historical explanations for the rural Korean habit of borrowing—or taking—first and then asking permission afterwards.

The celebration of Easter itself is always the greatest thing in the church's year. And if in our rustic community the ceremonies lack something in elegance and our alleluias are a little off key, nothing is really lost. Like the woman who suckled her baby all the while that she was devoutly following the Stations of the Cross on Good Friday, our tinny bells clanged out with uninhibited fervour on Holy Saturday night. We have a big font, and we splash plenty of water at the paschal baptisms. No service that we ever have matches the dramatic intensity of the dark church suddenly filled with many candles lighting the faces of the people in commemoration of the smashing of the gates of death during that holy night. By comparison to the ancient and elemental symbolism of this great service, the watery sentimentality of modern sunrise services is a weak thing indeed.

The Christians of my church converge from distant villages

en masse for this event, and their accommodation is always a problem. They bring their own food, and throughout Saturday afternoon there was a constant stream of people depositing bundles of rice in front of the altar as they paid their first visit to the church on arrival. Among them came a recently converted sorceress, some of whose repudiated instruments, a trident, a gong, and some cabalistic writings on sackcloth, are still in my room. Like many others, she brought a gift of eggs for the parish priest, most of them already hard-boiled. I set off gaily telling them of the appropriateness of eggs at Easter, of the coming of life from the apparently inanimate, of the simple symbolism of the broken shell for the shattered tomb. Only later did I discover that dyed and hard-boiled eggs were once part of the keeping of the Cold Food Festival.

Now Easter is over and spring is here. The warmth and the familiar spring winds induce a well-known seasonal lassitude, but men's minds are turning to thoughts of work. The heavy rain of Easter night has flooded some of the paddies and got some of the farmers out beginning to restore the baulks with mud. The barley is growing fast and making the dry fields look green and cheerful. Already many seeds are in, and we are in the midst of ploughing. Very soon the farmers' band from Chestnut Village, which woke me early on Good Friday morning as it came over the hills seeing one of the boys off for army service again, will be playing in earnest to alleviate the year's most strenuous labours.

The village enjoys spring, but behind the flowers and the sunshine and the building it senses the lurking spectres of the lean season and summer's hard work.

POSTSCRIPT

It is two years since I left Anjung, and a village does not stand still, least of all Anjung.

The interloping heretical conventicle has been torn down—by enraged villagers, I am told. A cinema with a beaten earth floor has grown up huge and ugly near the church. There are more houses, and the schools have expanded their buildings.

Most of the girls of my congregation have left the village to get married, and news comes now and then of their first babies or their miscarriages. Poor mad Agnes is dead; she suffocated on a hot summer day when they shut her up to keep her out of harm's way. Old T'aekhwa is very frail and has retired to a son's house in a poor suburb of Seoul. The bishop has ordained Elijah as an auxiliary priest, and Michael is now the father of a family with no visible means of support. One of the dancing boys has gone back to his brother, who is relieved and delighted. Another, after settling down as errand boy to old Naeng at the Chinese chop-house in Anjung, is now working in a bar in one of Seoul's red-light districts. Some of the high-school boys who were shy and gawky on the muddy lanes when I first knew them were in the forefront of the April 1960 revolution and have joined the intelligentsia of the capital.

Two years is in some ways a long time in Korea these days, because people's lives change rapidly whether they are old or young. Especially do they change for the people of places like Anjung, the villages that most feel the pinch of the grim hardness of Korean country life. But the pinch does not change.

AUTHOR'S NOTE

The Chinese characters for the names of the months used as chapter titles are taken from the traditional literary names of coincident lunar months that are still frequently used by the rural scholars in their letter writing. Their meaning is:

February	新元	New Beginning
March	春和	Spring Harmony
April	花雨	Flower Rain
May	梅雨	Plum Blossom Rain
June	麥秋	Barley Harvest
July	霖熱	Monsoon Heat
August	老炎	Waning Heat
September	秋涼	Autumn Cool
October	菊秋	Chrysanthemum Autumn
November	初寒	Beginning of Cold Weather
December	至寒	Bitter Cold
January	雪冱	Snow and Ice
February	春寒	Spring Cold
March	仲春	Full Spring
April	季春	The Last of Spring